# Vocabulary Power Plus
## for the New SAT:

Vocabulary, Reading, and Writing Exercises for High Scores

## Book Three

By Daniel A. Reed

Edited by Paul Moliken

ISBN 10:   1-58049-255-X
ISBN 13:  978-1-58049-255-3

**PRESTWICK HOUSE, INC.**
*"Everything for the English Classroom!"*

P.O. Box 658 • Clayton, DE 19938
(800) 932-4593 • www.prestwickhouse.com

# Table of Contents

# INTRODUCTION

Vocabulary Power Plus for the New SAT combines classroom-tested vocabulary drills with reading and writing exercises designed to prepare students for the revised Scholastic Assessment Test; however, Vocabulary Power Plus for the New SAT is a resource for all students—not just those who are college bound or preparing for the SAT I. This series is intended to increase vocabulary, improve grammar, enhance writing, and boost critical reading skills for students at all levels of learning.

Critical Reading exercises include lengthy passages and detailed questions. We use SAT-style grammar and writing exercises and have placed the vocabulary words in a non-alphabetical sequence.

To reflect the changes to the Writing and Critical Reading portions of the SAT I, Prestwick House includes inferential exercises instead of the analogical reasoning sections. Coupled with words-in-context activities, inferences cultivate comprehensive word discernment by prompting students to create contexts for words instead of simply memorizing definitions.

The writing exercises in Vocabulary Power Plus for the New SAT are process-oriented, but they bring students a step closer to SAT success by exposing them to rubrics that simulate those of the SAT essay-writing component. This exposure to an objective scoring process helps students to develop a concrete understanding of writing fundamentals.

We hope that you find the Vocabulary Power Plus for the New SAT series to be an effective tool for teaching new words and an exceptional tool for preparing for the new SAT.

# Strategies for Completing Activities

## Roots, Prefixes, and Suffixes

A knowledge of roots, prefixes, and suffixes can give readers the ability to view unfamiliar words as puzzles that require only a few simple steps to solve. For the person interested in the history of words, this knowledge provides the ability to track word origin and evolution. For those who seek was to improve vocabulary, this knowledge creates a sure and lifelong method; however, there are two points to remember:

1. Some words have evolved through usage, so present definitions might differ from what you infer through an examination of the roots and prefixes. The word *abstruse*, for example, contains the prefix *ab* (away) and the root *trudere* (to thrust), and literally means *to thrust away*. Today, *abstruse* is used to describe something that is hard to understand.

2. Certain roots do not apply to all words that use the same form. If you know that the root *vin* means "to conquer," then you would be correct in concluding that the word *invincible* means "incapable of being conquered;" however, if you tried to apply the same root meaning to *vindicate* or *vindictive*, you would be incorrect. When analyzing unfamiliar words, check for other possible roots if your inferred meaning does not fit the context.

Despite these considerations, a knowledge of roots and prefixes is one of the best ways to build a powerful vocabulary.

## Critical Reading

Reading questions generally fall into several categories.

1. *Identifying the main idea or the author's purpose.* Generally, the question will ask, "What is this selection about?"

In some passages, the author's purpose will be easy to identify because the one or two ideas leap from the text; however, other passages might not be so easily analyzed, especially if they include convoluted sentences. Inverted sentences (subject at end of sentence) and elliptical sentences (words missing) will also increase the difficulty of the passages, but all of these obstacles can be overcome if readers take one sentence at a time and recast it in their own words. Consider the following sentence:

These writers either jot down their thoughts bit by bit, in short, ambiguous, and paradoxical sentences, which apparently mean much more than they say—of this kind of writing Schelling's treatises on natural philosophy are a splendid instance; or else they hold forth with a deluge of words and the most intolerable diffusiveness, as though no end of fuss were necessary to make the reader understand the deep meaning of their sentences, whereas it is some quite simple if not actually trivial idea, examples of which may be found in plenty in the popular works of Fichte, and the philosophical manuals of a hundred other miserable dunces.

If we edit out some of the words, the main point of this sentence is obvious.

These writers either jot down their thoughts bit by bit, in short,
sentences, which apparently mean much
more than they say
or they hold
a deluge of words as
though necessary to make the reader understand
the deep meaning of their sentences

Some sentences need only a few deletions for clarification, but others require major recasting and additions; they must be read carefully and put into the reader's own words.

Some in their discourse desire rather commendation of wit, in being able to hold all arguments, than of judgment, in discerning what is true; as if it were a praise to know what might be said, and not what should be thought.

After studying it, a reader might recast the sentence as follows:

In conversation, some people desire praise for their abilities to maintain the conversation rather than their abilities to identify what is true or false, as though it were better to sound good than to know what is truth or fiction.

2.  Identifying the stated or inferred meaning. *What is the author stating or suggesting?*

The literal meaning of a text does not always correspond with the intended meaning. To fully understand a passage, readers must determine which meaning—if there is more than one—is the intended meaning of the passage.

Consider the following sentence:

> If his notice was sought, an expression of courtesy and interest gleamed out upon his features; proving that there was light within him and that it was only the outward medium of the intellectual lamp that obstructed the rays in their passage.

Interpreted literally, this Nathaniel Hawthorne metaphor suggests that a light-generating lamp exists inside the human body. Since this is impossible, the reader must look to the metaphoric meaning of the passage to properly understand it. In the metaphor, Hawthorne refers to the human mind—consciousness—as a lamp that emits light, and other people cannot always see the lamp because the outside "medium"—the human body—sometimes blocks it.

3.  Identifying the tone or mood of the selection. *What feeling does the text evoke?*

To answer these types of questions, readers must look closely at individual words and their connotations; for example, the words *stubborn* and *firm* share almost the same definition, but a writer who describes a character as *stubborn* rather than *firm* is probably suggesting something negative about the character.

## Writing

The new SAT allocates only twenty-five minutes to the composition of a well-organized, fully developed essay. Writing a satisfactory essay in this limited time requires the ability to quickly determine a thesis, organize ideas, and produce adequate examples to support the ideas.

An essay written in twenty minutes might not represent the best process writing—an SAT essay might lack the perfection and depth that weeks of proofreading and editing give to research papers. Process is undoubtedly important, but students must consider the time constraints of the SAT. Completion of the essay is just as important as organization, development, and language use.

The thesis, the organization of ideas, and the support make the framework of a good essay. Before the actual writing begins, writers must create a mental outline by establishing a thesis, or main idea, and one or more specific supporting ideas (the number of ideas will depend on the length and content of the essay). Supporting ideas should not be overly complicated; they are simply ideas that justify or explain the thesis. The writer must introduce and explain each supporting idea, and the resultant supporting paragraph should answer the *why?* or *who cares?* questions that the thesis evokes.

Once the thesis and supporting ideas are identified, writers must determine the order in which the ideas will appear in the essay. A good introduction usually explains the thesis and briefly introduces the supporting ideas. Explanation of the supporting ideas should follow, with each idea in its own paragraph. The final paragraph, the conclusion, usually restates the thesis or summarizes the main ideas of the essay.

Adhering to the mental outline when the writing begins will help the writer organize and develop the essay. Using the Organization and Development scoring guides to evaluate practice essays will help to reinforce the process skills. The Word Choice and Sentence Formation scoring guides will help to strengthen language skills—the vital counterpart to essay organization and development.

# Pronunciation Guide

a — track
ā — mate
ä — father
â — care
e — pet
ē — be
i — bit
ī — bite
o — job
ō — wrote
ô — port, horse, **fought**
ōō — proof
ŏŏ — book
u — pun
ū — **you**
û — purr
ə — about, system, supper, circus
îr — steer
ë — Fr. coeur
oi — toy

# Word List

## Lesson 1
aegis
altruism
amorphous
besiege
boor
carrion
enervate
ephemeral
erotic
factious
fervent
ignoble
opulent
perspicacity
rectify

## Lesson 2
antithesis
bauble
bestial
bland
chagrin
diaphanous
effete
emendation
gloat
impediment
impotent
labyrinth
maelstrom
nihilism
shard

## Lesson 3
adventitious
ambiguous
bona fide
cataclysm
deviate
edify
extenuate
fecund
glower
impale
importune
obfuscate
optimum
parochial
pedestrian

## Lesson 4
baroque
besmirch
celibate
debacle
demeanor
facetious
fortuitous
hedonism
imperative
obloquy
perfunctory
quasi-
recapitulate
sacrosanct
sadistic

## Lesson 5
bowdlerize
carnal
deference
ebullient
elegy
fop
impair
imprecation
nebulous
non sequitur
panegyric
pedantic
quandary
rakish
sanguine

## Lesson 6
affluence
amoral
antipathy
banal
bedlam
denouement
elucidate
eschew
imminent
obdurate
onerous
parody
peruse
scurrilous
sedulous

Lesson 7
adroit
affectation
bovine
callow
dichotomy
fatuous
ferret
knell
laconic
macroscopic
patent
peccadillo
quiddity
rationalize
sagacious

Lesson 8
agape
carcinogen
censure
deride
gambol
gibe
grotesque
hackneyed
immolate
imperious
martinet
neologism
olfactory
quagmire
recondite

Lesson 9
blanch
chimerical
eclectic
finesse
grandiose
harbinger
heterogeneous
hybrid
idiosyncrasy
machination
masochist
nubile
pejorative
raiment
sapient

Lesson 10
adulterate
bucolic
caveat
defile
diadem
emanate
garish
gratuitous
idolatry
immutable
impecunious
impious
onus
redolent
sedition

Lesson 11
cessation
delineate
desiccated
elixir
epitome
fetish
fissure
garrulous
juxtapose
kinetic
lachrymose
languid
legerdemain
libertine
scintillate

Lesson 12
badinage
bilious
blandishment
debauchery
fastidious
garner
gumption
halcyon
hegira
kismet
malapropism
milieu
necromancy
paradigm
regress

| Lesson 19 | Lesson 20 | Lesson 21 |
|-----------|-----------|-----------|
| abnegation | acerbic | bon mot |
| acrid | androgynous | clandestine |
| apex | augur | digress |
| credulity | beatitude | furlough |
| dross | diaspora | misogyny |
| fulminate | discursive | peon |
| gravitas | disseminate | plenary |
| hegemony | extemporaneous | plutocrat |
| insuperable | intractable | potboiler |
| jejune | maladroit | redoubtable |
| polyglot | politic | stolid |
| psychosomatic | requiem | succor |
| truculent | sinecure | travesty |
| verisimilitude | tendentious | vignette |
| viscous | traduce | xeric |

# Lesson One

1.  **factious** (fak´ shəs) *adj.* causing disagreement
    The *factious* sailors refused to sail any farther into the storm.
    *syn: belligerent; contentious*           *ant: cooperative; united*

2.  **ignoble** (ig nō´ bəl) *adj.* dishonorable; shameful
    Cheating on an exam is an *ignoble* way to get good grades.
    *syn: despicable; base*           *ant: noble; glorious*

3.  **boor** (bôr) *n.* a rude or impolite person
    The *boor* grabbed handfuls of hors d'oeuvres and walked around while he ate them.
    *syn: buffoon; clown*           *ant: sophisticate*

4.  **aegis** (ē´ jis) *n.* a shield; protection
    The life of the witness is under the *aegis* of the witness protection program.
    *syn: backing*

5.  **perspicacity** (pûr spi kas´ i tē) *n.* keenness of judgment
    The old hermit still had the *perspicacity* to haggle with the automotive dealer.
    *syn: perceptiveness*           *ant: stupidity; ignorance*

6.  **fervent** (fûr´ vənt) *adj.* eager; earnest
    We made a *fervent* attempt to capture the stallion, but he was too quick for us.
    *syn: burning; passionate*           *ant: apathetic*

7.  **rectify** (rek´ tə fī) *v.* to correct; to make right
    JoAnne tried to *rectify* her poor relationship with her son by spending more time with him.
    *syn: remedy; resolve*

8.  **enervate** (en´ ər vāt) *v.* to weaken
    The record temperatures *enervated* the farmhands before noon.
    *syn: devitalize; exhaust*           *ant: energize; strengthen*

9. **besiege** (bi sēj´) *v.* to overwhelm; to surround and attack
People jumped from the ground and brushed themselves off as ants *besieged* the picnic.

10. **ephemeral** (i fem´ ər əl) *adj.* lasting only a brief time; short-lived
The gardener experienced *ephemeral* fame the year she grew a half-ton pumpkin.
*syn: transient; fleeting*          *ant: permanent*

11. **altruism** (al´ trōō iz əm) *n.* a concern for others; generosity
A person with *altruism* will usually stop and help a stranded motorist.
*syn: unselfishness; magnanimity*      *ant: selfishness; egoism*

12. **carrion** (kar´ ē ən) *n.* decaying flesh
The *carrion* along the desert highway was a feast for the vultures.

13. **erotic** (i rot´ ik) *adj.* pertaining to sexual love
The museum staff cancelled the exhibition when it saw the *erotic* sculptures.

14. **amorphous** (ə môr´ fəs) *adj.* shapeless, formless, vague
What began as an *amorphous* idea in Steven's dream turned into a revolutionary way to power automobiles.

15. **opulent** (op´ ū lənt) *adj.* rich, luxurious; wealthy
Despite the stock market crash, the wealthy family continued its *opulent* lifestyle.

## EXERCISE I—Words in Context

*From the list below, supply the words needed to complete the paragraph. Some words will not be used.*

amorphous     enervate     besiege     factious
ephemeral     perspicacity     altruism     carrion

1.     Carter had been walking for more than four hours since his truck ran out of fuel. The morning desert sun _____ him, bringing him closer to exhaustion. In his weary state, he chastised himself for not having the _____ to have brought an extra can of fuel on the trip. In such a barren, isolated place, Carter knew that he couldn't rely on the _____ of others for help if his truck broke down. The only living things on the road were biting flies that _____ Carter and forced him to swat his face and neck every few seconds. They continued to attack until they detected the foul smell of _____ when Carter passed a dead hare on the shoulder of the road. The departure of the flies gave him _____ relief as he continued his trudge; the bugs went away, but in the distance, Carter could see, through eyes stinging with sweat, the _____ distortions of light along the hot, desert floor.

*From the list below, supply the words needed to complete the paragraph. Some words will not be used.*

rectify     factious     ignoble     erotic     amorphous     besiege

2.     Some of the council approved the new zoning restriction, but a few _____ members refused to cast votes. None of them actually approved of the _____ bookstore next to the little league field, but they wanted to find a better way to legally _____ the _____ situation.

*From the list below, supply the words needed to complete the paragraph. Some words will not be used.*

aegis    altruism    boor    fervent    carrion    opulent

3.    Councilman Parker, a wealthy native of the small town, knew that a few council members had a[n] _____ desire to remove him from office. Some of them resented his _____ lifestyle, and others claimed that Parker was careless because he lived under the _____ of his wealth and thus had no fear of being fired. They also called Parker a _____ because he had the habit of interrupting conversations and barging into offices without knocking.

## EXERCISE II—Sentence Completion

*Complete the sentence in a way that shows you understand the meaning of the italicized vocabulary word.*

1.    The highway crew removed the *carrion* from the road because…

2.    Bob decided to *rectify* his crime by…

3.    People called Cory a *boor* because he always…

4.    In an act of *altruism*, Jennifer went to the nursing home to…

5.    Citizens protested the opening of an *erotic* bookstore near the park because…

6.    Under the *aegis* of the police department, the witness could safely…

7.    During the summit, the *factious* ambassador caused…

8.    Working on the roof *enervated* the contractors, especially when…

9.    The *ephemeral* argument was over in…

10.    Features in the *opulent* mansion include…

11.    The wounded fish was soon *besieged* by…

12. The *amorphous* body of the amoeba had no discernable…

13. If it were not for dad's *perspicacity*, I would have purchased a car that…

14. His *fervent* speech convinced…

15. A person can lose his or her job by committing an *ignoble* act such as…

## EXERCISE III—Roots, Prefixes, and Suffixes

*Study the entries and answer the questions that follow.*

> The roots *fus* and *fun* mean "melt" or "pour out."
> The suffix *ion* means "the act of."
> The roots *grad* and *gress* means "step" or "go."
> The suffix *el* means "little."
> The prefix *con* means "together."
> The prefixes *di*, *dif*, and *dis* mean "apart."
> The prefix *e* means "out" or "from."

1. Using literal translations as guidance, define the following words without using a dictionary.

   A. fusion
   B. funnel
   C. infuse

   D. regress
   E. progress
   F. congress

2. If you have an *effusive* personality, then it _____ of you.
   Motor oil will _____ across the gravel if it spills out of the can.

3. A step-by-step process is often called a[n] _____ process, and a highway crew might use a[n] _____ to smooth out a road.

4. *Egress* literally translates to _____, and if someone loses a high-paying job and takes a lower-paying job, his or her career is said to have _____.

5. List all the words that you can think of that contain the roots *grad* and *gress*.

## EXERCISE IV—Inference

*Complete the sentences by inferring information about the italicized word from its context.*

1. You probably will not miss too many days of school, because the *ephemeral* strain of influenza does not...

2. Brenda felt guilty for stealing the money from the register, so she *rectified* the situation by...

3. Out of pure *altruism*, Ed went to the homeless shelter on Christmas Eve to...

## Exercise V—Writing

*Here is a writing prompt similar to the one you will find on the writing portion of the SAT:*

Plan and write an essay based on the following statement:

> Passing judgment on nontraditional families seems to be customary for what Barbara Kingsolver calls "the Family of Dolls," the traditional Barbie and Ken household that has never been disassembled by divorce. The ever-ambiguous "family values" suggests that traditional families offer the most stability for children, nurturing them in a community of successful relationships from which they can model their own lives. Divorced people, gay families, *Brady Bunch* families, and single parents put their children at risk and are failures.
>
> Adapted from "Stone Soup" by Barbara Kingsolver.

**Assignment:** Write an essay in which you support or refute Barbara Kingsolver's position. Be certain to support your own position with examples from literature, current events, or your own personal experience or observation.

**Thesis:** Write a one-sentence response to the above assignment. Make certain this single sentence offers a clear statement of your position.

*Example: In a nation where non-traditional families are beginning to outnumber nuclear families, reorganized families are as successful as nuclear families in raising capable, thriving children who are at no more risk for failure than children from traditional families.*

**Organizational Plan:** If your thesis is the point on which you want to end, where does your essay need to begin? List the points of development that are inevitable in leading your reader from your beginning point to your end point. This is your outline.

**Draft:** Use your thesis as both your beginning and your end. Following your outline, write a good first draft of your essay. Remember to support all your points with examples, facts, references to reading, etc.

**Review and revise:** Exchange essays with a classmate. Using the scoring guide for Organization on page 240, score your partner's essay (while he or she scores yours). Focus on the organizational plan and use of language conventions. If necessary, rewrite your essay to improve the organizational plan and/or your use of language.

## Identifying Sentence Errors

*Identify the grammatical error in each of the following sentences. If the sentence contains no error, select answer choice E.*

1. The <u>mechanic repairs</u>  <u>not only</u>  <u>domestic</u> cars but also <u>he repairs</u>
      (A)             (B)      (C)                (D)
    foreign cars.    <u>No error</u>
                       (E)

2. The <u>clients requested</u> information on <u>what</u> factors would <u>effect</u> the
      (A)                      (B)           (C)
    interest that they would earn on <u>their</u> stocks.    <u>No error</u>
                          (D)        (E)

3. My mother finds it peculiar <u>that while I</u>, and most of my female
                           (A)
    friends <u>would do</u> just about anything to get a taste of something sweet,
         (B)
    <u>my brother</u> and his friends <u>wait for dinner to eat</u>.    <u>No error</u>
       (C)                    (D)         (E)

4. Through language, stereotypes and standards <u>are</u> communicated
                                    (A)
    <u>to those who</u> are required to listen<u>: therefore</u>, schools are a medium
    (B)                         (C)
    through  which the population <u>is controlled.</u>    <u>No error</u>
                      (D)       (E)

5. The government, <u>who attempt</u> to use welfare <u>as a means of</u> controlling
          (A)                (B)
    social classes, <u>is ignoring</u> the <u>inherent</u> problems of the system.    <u>No error</u>
              (C)      (D)                    (E)

## Improving Sentences

*The underlined portion of each sentence below contains some flaw. Select the answer choice that best corrects the flaw.*

6. The first baseman forgot to take his glove to the field, <u>and he stops in the middle of the inning to retrieve his mitt.</u>
   A. and he is stopping in the middle of the inning to retrieve his mitt.
   B. and he stopped in the middle of the inning to retrieve his mitt.
   C. and he leaves in the middle of the inning to retrieve his mitt.
   D. and he stopped in the middle of the inning, retrieving his mitt.
   E. and he is stopping in the middle of the inning, retrieving his mitt.

7. <u>Clearing the bar at seven feet, a new high jump record was set.</u>
   A. A new high jump record was set, while clearing the bar at seven feet.
   B. While clearing the bar at seven feet, a new high jump record was set.
   C. A new high jump record was set when the athlete cleared the bar at seven feet.
   D. A new high jump record, by clearing the bar seven feet, was set.
   E. After clearing the bar at seven feet, a new high jump record was set.

8. <u>The athlete was acclaimed for her performance.</u>
   A. Acclaimed for her performance was the athlete.
   B. The athlete was acclaimed for her performance by the judges.
   C. By the judges, the athlete was acclaimed for her performance.
   D. The judges acclaimed the athlete for her performance.
   E. The judges acclaimed the performance for the athlete.

9. <u>The college student enjoys swimming and to write but not studying.</u>
   A. The college student enjoys swimming and to write but not to study.
   B. The college student enjoys swimming, and to write, but not to study.
   C. Enjoying swimming and to write but not to study, the college student spends her day.
   D. The college student enjoys to swim and to write but not to study.
   E. The college student enjoys swimming and writing but not studying.

10. <u>The musical was exceptional, the cast was only mediocre.</u>
    A. Though the musical was exceptional, the cast was only mediocre.
    B. The musical was exceptional, the cast is only mediocre.
    C. The musical was exceptional because the cast was only mediocre.
    D. The musical was exceptional, if only the cast was mediocre.
    E. The musical was exceptional, or the cast was only mediocre.

# Lesson Two

1. **impotent** (im´ pə tənt) *adj.* powerless; lacking strength
   Without the gun, he felt *impotent*.
   *syn: ineffective; helpless*            *ant: potent; powerful*

2. **antithesis** (an tith´ i sis) *n.* an exact opposite; an opposite extreme
   Love is the *antithesis* of hate.
   *syn: converse*            *ant: same*

3. **maelstrom** (māl´ strəm) *n.* whirlpool; turbulence; agitated state of mind
   His emotions were like a *maelstrom,* and he couldn't decide what course to follow.

4. **emendation** (ē´men dā´ shən) *n.* a correction
   The last edition of the book contains many *emendations*.
   *syn: improvement; amendment*

5. **chagrin** (shə grin´) *n.* embarrassment; a complete loss of courage
   Joanne had never felt such *chagrin* as when she fell into the mud puddle in front of her fiancé's family.

6. **bauble** (bô´ bəl) *n.* a showy but useless thing
   John had to find some kind of *bauble* to give Mary for Christmas.
   *syn: trinket*

7. **diaphanous** (dī af´ ə nəs) *adj.* very sheer and light
   The *diaphanous* gown was beautiful, but Gloria wasn't sure she had the nerve to wear it.
   *syn: transparent; gossamer*            *ant: opaque*

8. **labyrinth** (lab´ ə rinth) *n.* a complicated network of winding passages; a maze
   The mice were made to run through a *labyrinth* in order to reach their food.

9. **gloat** (glōt) *v.* to look at or think about with great satisfaction
   The track team *gloated* over their latest victory.
   *syn: revel; crow*

10. **impediment** (im ped´ ə mənt) *n.* a barrier; obstruction
    The supervisor wouldn't be an *impediment* to her advancement.
    *syn: obstacle; hindrance*            *ant: aid*

11. **bestial** (bes´ chəl) *adj.* savage; brutal
    He took a *bestial* delight in tormenting the captive slaves.
    *syn: brutish; vile; cruel*          *ant: humane; kind*

12. **effete** (e fēt´) *adj.* worn out; barren
    Although worn down by age and a life of hard work, the man was far from *effete*.
    *syn: exhausted; spent and sterile*          *ant: vital; vigorous*

13. **shard** (shärd) *n.* a fragment
    The doctor pulled a *shard* of glass from the girl's arm.

14. **bland** (bland) *adj.* mild; tasteless; dull
    His *bland* manner had a calming effect on the children.
    *syn: smooth; agreeable*          *ant: exciting; thrilling*

15. **nihilism** (nī´ ə liz´əm) *n.* a total rejection of established laws
    *Nihilism* rejects established laws and order, but it offers nothing in their place.

## EXERCISE I—Words in Context

*From the list below, supply the words needed to complete the paragraph. Some words will not be used.*

| | | | |
|---|---|---|---|
| impotent | bestial | maelstrom | antithesis |
| impediment | emendation | chagrin | labyrinth |
| diaphanous | gloat | | |

1.      Loren, the new manager, is the _____ of compassion; just yesterday, she fired two people because they were late to work once this week. Corporate headquarters, upset with declining sales, appointed Loren to replace a[n] _____ manager who had been spotted on the golf course during work hours one-too-many times.

Loren's many changes and _____ to company guidelines caused a[n] _____ in both the warehouse and the salesroom. Employees faced evaluations and new instructions that drove many to resign; however, it was all just a part of Loren's plan. The people who quit, she reasoned, were just _____ to meeting the expected monthly profit margin.

Loren spent the first two weeks familiarizing herself with the _____ of shelves and palettes in the warehouse. Shreds of textiles littered parts of the packaging area; some were hefty snippets of wool, and others were _____ scraps of silk that hovered in the gust created by passing forklifts. She occasionally stopped to introduce herself to the workers, but she ceased her introductions after noticing the regular look of _____ on workers' faces as they scrambled to look busy or stumbled over the proper responses to her questions. After the first round of resignations and firings, most of the workers were intimidated by Loren's _____ management techniques.

From the list below, supply the words needed to complete the paragraph. Some words will not be used.

| | | | |
|---|---|---|---|
| bauble | bland | shard | nihilism |
| labyrinth | effete | gloat | bestial |

2.    Most of the office personnel assumed that Devon's home life was as _____ as his uninteresting manner at work. Reserved and soft spoken, Devon sat at a desk every day filling out purchase orders and staring at the only ornamental object on his desk: a glass paperweight with a brass tag commemorating fifteen years of service—a[n] _____ presented to Devon by the company in lieu of a bonus or a raise. It must not have been very sentimental to Devon, because he did not say a word when one of the interns accidentally knocked the glass bubble to the floor, where the _____ still can be heard crunching beneath the wheels of antiquated office chairs.

    The passing years took a toll on Devon's unremarkable body. In the months following the fall of the paperweight, he developed a weary look, _____ from the exhausting monotony of filling out purchase orders for fifteen years. Occasionally, in the break room, he listened to some of the younger workers _____ about how quickly they were promoted; most were at least ten years younger than Devon and had half the experience. A hidden rage boiled within Devon every time he overheard the familiar brag of a new, young manager. The promotions were prime examples of _____ in the company, he reasoned; "I've got the seniority, not those kids," he'd mumble to himself, but never loud enough for anyone to hear.

# EXERCISE II—Sentence Completion

*Complete the sentence in a way that shows you understand the meaning of the italicized vocabulary word.*

1. People knew that Jimmy practiced *nihilism* when he...

2. Todd's parents did not hide their *chagrin* after their son...

3. Heidi's friends did not want to hear her *gloat* about...

4. *Shards* of broken taillights littered the highway after...

5. The crowd knew that the *impotent* boxer would not be able to...

6. When Dave submitted a term paper that required *emendations*, the teacher...

7. Mary scolded Bert for wasting money on useless *baubles*, such as...

8. Ashley was suspended for wearing a *diaphanous* shirt to...

9. The mall is a *labyrinth*, so check the map or you will...

10. Vicky caused a *maelstrom* of panic when she told everyone that...

11. Chrissie is the *antithesis* of Ben, because she is friendly to strangers while he...

12. The largest *impediment* to crossing the river is...

13. Your dinner will taste *bland* if you do not...

14. The team must change its *effete* stratergy if...

15. The soldier endured *bestial* treatment after...

## EXERCISE III—Roots, Prefixes, and Suffixes

*Study the entries and answer the questions that follow.*

The root *somn* means "sleep."
The root *pot* means "to drink."
The root *vac* means "empty."
The root *sid* means "to sit" or "to settle."
The prefix *e* means "out" or "completely."
The prefix *in* means "not."
The prefix *dis* means "not" or "apart."
The prefix *pre* means "before" or "in front of."

1. Using literal translations as guidance, define the following words without using a dictionary.

   A   evacuate             D.   dissenter
   B.   vacate              E.   reside
   C.   potation            F.   president

2. A magic drink is often called a[n] _____.

   Water from the stream will not be _____, or drinkable, until you boil it.

3. If you cannot sleep, then you might have a condition called _____.

   *Somnolent* music might help you to _____.

4. *Insidious* literally translates to "sitting in," but the word means "secretly working to cause harm." Explain the possible connection between the actual and literal definitions of *insidious*.

5. List as many words as you can think of that contain the root *sid*.

## EXERCISE IV—Inference

*Complete the sentences by inferring information about the italicized word from its context.*

1.  If Larry *gloated* about his skills after the last bowling tournament, then one can probably assume that…

2.  Sometime Nikki wakes up too early because the *diaphanous* curtains over the bedroom windows do not…

3.  Keith scolded the children, but then he felt immense *chagrin* when his wife told him that the damage to the car was…

## EXERCISE V—Critical Reading

*Below is a reading passage followed by several multiple-choice questions similar to the ones you will encounter on the SAT. Carefully read the passage and choose the best answer for each of the questions.*

*The following passage describes one of the worst man-made disasters in United States history. More than two thousand people died in the Johnstown Flood of 1889 when the South Fork Dam failed.*

The morning of May 31st, 1889, was not an average morning for the thirty thousand citizens of Johnstown, Pennsylvania, but it was not a particularly exceptional morning, either. Heavy rains during the night had caused the Little Conemaugh River to spill over its banks, but mild flooding was not uncommon for the growing
5   steel town. People went about their daily business among the sounds of clanging train cars, trotting horses, and clinking machinery of the iron works. All those sounds would soon be drowned in an ominous rumble from the hills north of town.

South Fork Dam, fourteen miles north of Johnstown, retained the water of Lake Conemaugh high in the Allegheny Mountains. The dam, built in 1831, created the
10   two-mile lake, which served as a reservoir for the Pennsylvania Mainline Canal; however, railways soon rendered the canal obsolete, and the Pennsylvania Railroad purchased the canal from the state. The railroad operated parts of the canal until the dam failed in 1862 while the lake was half full. The railroad sold Lake Conemaugh to a congressman, who removed the dam's discharge system and sold
15   it for scrap. He then sold the property to Benjamin Ruff of the South Fork Fishing and Hunting Club, and in 1879, Mr. Ruff made repairs to the dam and constructed a pleasure community around Lake Conemaugh. For ten years, the club served as a successful resort for Pittsburgh's elite, including Andrew Carnegie and Andrew Mellon.

20   While people in Johnstown went about their daily routines on the morning after the storm, the caretakers of the South Fork Fishing and Hunting Club scrambled to deal with a lake that was rapidly rising to dangerous levels. Everyone in the Little Conemaugh River valley, included the citizens of Johnstown, had joked about the condition of the dam for years. They speculated about the day that it would finally
25   burst, but few actually worried about it. When the water of Lake Conemaugh approached the top of the dam, the workers in South Fork knew that it was time to worry.

After the heavy rain, approximately ten thousand cubic feet of water entered Lake Conemaugh each hour, but only six thousand cubic feet escaped over the
30   spillway. In the morning, the lake was only two feet from the top of the dam, and it was still rising. Workers hurriedly cleaned tons of debris from spillways to let more water escape, but the lake continued to rise. A team of laborers dug a trench to route water around the dam, but the ditch was too shallow to have any great effect. Inch by inch, the water neared the top of the dam, and at noon, it began to
35   wash away the earthen structure. By two o'clock, the rushing water had cut through the top center of the dam, but most of the lake was still contained. At three o'clock, Lake Conemaugh—twenty million tons of water—burst through the center of the dam.

Workers in South Fork sent telegraph warnings to Johnstown when the lake
40  began to spill over the dam, but most of the residents dismissed them. People who
actually took the warnings seriously and left for high ground were ridiculed by
those who remained in town.

It took forty-five minutes for Lake Conemaugh to rush through the broken dam,
and in that time it became a frothing torrent—a forty-foot wall of water that flat-
45  tened everything in its path. The wave, on a downhill course to Johnstown, grew in
mass as it picked up trees, rocks, and chunks of debris. By four o'clock, the people
of Johnstown noticed that the river had become strangely rapid, and in the minutes
that followed, they heard a strange rumble in the distance.

The wall of water hit Johnstown at 4:07 p.m. Neither wood nor iron slowed it
50  down. It swept away buildings as though they were made of balsa wood. The heavy
debris that it picked up gave the wave the properties of a mace that easily smashed
though any manmade obstacle. Brick walls shattered, and steel railroad cars tum-
bled like children's toys. Not even the most permanent of structures proved to be
heavy enough to protect people from the water. People who were swept away bat-
55  tled to stay afloat and alive; some were crushed by debris, and others, hiding in the
attics of their homes, drowned when the wave dragged their homes from their foun-
dations.

In ten minutes, four square miles of downtown area had been completely oblit-
erated. Though the initial wave had passed, a swift current, twenty-feet deep, still
60  flowed through the city. Those people lucky enough to have taken cover on solid
buildings stood on rooftops and nervously watched as the floodwaters consumed
nearby buildings. Hundreds of people were missing, and approximately five hundred were trapped in a massive pile of debris that the wave had deposited against a
bridge. The twisted heap, more than forty-acres in area, contained homes, bridges,
65  railroad cars, and machines from Johnstown and four other communities along the
Little Conemaugh. People crawled from the entanglement and struggled to find
high ground, but not everyone made it to safety before the debris, soaked with oil
from an overturned train car, caught fire. Eighty people perished in the flames.

Two thousand, two hundred nine people died as a result of the Johnstown Flood.
70  The destructive wave removed 99 families, 1600 homes, and 280 businesses from
the face of the earth. Unsanitary conditions, cholera, and missing family members
made matters worse in the days that followed, but luckily, a few good elements
sprouted from the destruction.

The disaster galvanized the nation, and nearly four million dollars in relief
75  money poured into Johnstown from the United States and eighteen foreign nations.
Hundreds of volunteers swarmed to the city to provide food, blankets, and tempo-
rary shelters for thousands of victims. The flood also prompted the first major disaster relief effort for the newly formed American Red Cross, which has helped
countless millions since. No one ever rebuilt the South Fork Dam, but the tragic
80  flood has forever changed the way in which people think about potential manmade
disasters.

1. The tone of the passage is best described as
   A. bitter and mournful.
   B. excited and nostalgic.
   C. spiteful but analytical.
   D. sober but heartening.
   E. cross and skeptical.

2. As used in line 7, *ominous* most nearly means
   A. loud.
   B. cautious.
   C. foreboding.
   D. roaring.
   E. singular.

3. According to the passage, how many times has the South Fork Dam broken since 1831?
   A. zero
   B. one
   C. two
   D. three
   E. four

4. According to the passage, the South Fork Dam was made of
   A. concrete.
   B. cement.
   C. steel.
   D. earth.
   E. bakelite.

5. Few people evacuated the city before the flood because
   A. Johnstown was accustomed to frequent floods.
   B. the telegraph wires were down.
   C. no one took the warning seriously.
   D. the men on horses did not reach the city soon enough.
   E. the engineer at South Fork told them not to worry.

6. The simile in line 50 emphasizes
   A. the popularity of model toys in Johnstown.
   B. the overwhelming force of the surge.
   C. that most hardwood trees survived the wave.
   D. the shoddy construction of buildings in the nineteenth century.
   E. that light wood is best used to build rafts.

7. In line 51, the word *mace* refers to
   A. a debilitating aerosol.
   B. a blinding spray.
   C. a fragrant spice.
   D. an attorney's clout.
   E. a heavy club.

8. When the surge hit Johnstown, how long did it take to destroy the downtown area?
   A. three minutes
   B. five minutes
   C. ten minutes
   D. twenty minutes
   E. forty-five minutes

9. Which of the following would be the most appropriate title for this passage?
   A. Life on the Flood Plain
   B. The Johnstown Flood of 1889
   C. Preventing Looting After Disasters
   D. Recovery Efforts After the Johnstown Flood
   E. The Dangers of Heavy Rain

10. This passage would probably be found in a[n]
    A. engineering magazine.
    B. social studies textbook.
    C. daily newspaper.
    D. book about early country clubs in the United States.
    E. American Red Cross pamphlet.

# Lesson Three

1. **pedestrian** (pə des´ trē ən)  *adj.*  ordinary or dull
   The crowd responded to the *pedestrian* speech with yawns.
   *syn: commonplace; mediocre*                    *ant: imaginative; compelling*

2. **bona fide** (bō´ nə fīd)  *adj.*  in good faith
   We made a *bona fide* offer for the property.
   *syn: legitimate; genuine*                    *ant: fraudulent; phony*

3. **adventitious** (ad´ ven tish´ əs)  *adj.*  accidental; nonessential
   The scientists admitted that the breakthrough was an *adventitious* result of
   the study.
   *syn: incidental*

4. **fecund** (fē´ kənd)  *adj.*  fertile; productive
   The *fecund* soil produced a record number of tomatoes this year.
   *syn: prolific*                    *ant: sterile*

5. **deviate** (dē´ vē āt)  *v.*  to turn aside from a course; to stray
   Sometimes it's better to *deviate* from the truth than to hurt someone's
   feelings.
   *syn: digress*

6. **obfuscate** (ob´ fus kāt)  *v.*  to confuse; to bewilder
   The realtor tried to *obfuscate* the issue, and it was working, because the
   confused buyer did not know if he was coming or going.
   *syn: muddle; obscure*                    *ant: clarify; elucidate*

7. **impale** (im pāl´)  *v.*  to pierce with a sharp stake through the body
   The natives used sharp sticks to *impale* fish in the tide pools.

8. **extenuate** (ek sten´ ū āt)  *v.*  to lessen seriousness by providing partial
   excuses
   The jury believes that the thief's situation *extenuates* the crime of stealing
   food.

9. **parochial** (pə rō´ kē əl)  *adj.*  local; narrow; limited
   Because he had never traveled outside his own town, Jim had a very
   *parochial* view of life.
   *syn: provincial; narrow-minded*                    *ant: universal; catholic*

10. **glower** (glou´ ər) *v.* to stare angrily
The boy *glowered* at his mother when she corrected his manners.
*syn: frown; scowl*                    *ant: grin*

11. **edify** (ed´ ə fī) *v.* improve someone morally
The sermon was meant to *edify* the congregation.

12. **ambiguous** (am big´ yōō əs) *adj.* open to more than one interpretation
The candidate's *ambiguous* comments tended to confuse the issue even more.
*syn: unclear; uncertain; vague*          *ant: explicit; definite*

13. **cataclysm** (kat´ ə kliz əm) *n.* a violent change
The earthquake in Mexico was a *cataclysm* which no one could have foreseen.
*syn: disaster; catastrophe*          *ant: triumph; boon*

14. **optimum** (op´ tə mum) *adj.* best; most favorable; ideal
The pilot was waiting for *optimum* conditions before setting out on the dangerous flight.

15. **importune** (im pôr tōōn´) *v.* to ask persistently; to beg
John *importuned* his father, but could not get the car keys.
*syn: appeal; badger*

## EXERCISE I—Words in Context

*From the list below, supply the words needed to complete the paragraph. Some words will not be used.*

|            |          |            |              |
|------------|----------|------------|--------------|
| deviate    | impale   | glower     | obfuscate    |
| cataclysm  | optimum  | pedestrian | adventitious |

1.    The _____, two-hour lecture only _____ the students. They respected the guest speaker's experience, but every time she _____ from the complex topic, she added ten _____ minutes to the harangue. The conditions of the auditorium were not _____ for long lectures; the air conditioner was broken, and the heat and poor lighting forced many of the students to fight drowsiness. One young man nearly _____ himself on a number two pencil when he nodded off while doodling in his notebook. He caught himself and quickly sat up straight; the speaker _____ at him for a few seconds, but never stopped speaking.

From the list below, supply the words needed to complete the paragraph. Some words will not be used.

| | | | | |
|---|---|---|---|---|
| bona fide | fecund | parochial | edify | impale |
| ambiguous | cataclysm | importune | extenuate | |

2.　　At the check-out line, Timmy _____ his mother to purchase a new brand of candy bar for him; however, her reaction was a[n] _____ compared to her usual tolerant reactions to Timmy's requests. Everyone stared when Lynn screamed at Timmy and told him to return the candy bar and stop whining because no, he doesn't need it.

　　Before she snapped in the grocery store, Lynn had concealed her anxiety for a week. The rent-check was later than it had ever been, and the landlord had a[n] _____ view in financial matters. Lynn had already bought an extra week by reassuring him of her _____ intention to pay the rent with her first paycheck, but the week had passed and she still hadn't found a job. The landlord had given her the usual speech about honoring a lease, apparently in an attempt to _____ Lynn; however, no matter what the landlord thought, Lynn felt that losing her job without warning _____ the extra time she needed to pay the rent. It was the landlord's _____ tone that really bothered her; Lynn couldn't be sure if the landlord would continue being compassionate or if he would send an eviction notice upon finding no rent payment in his mailbox that morning. Lynn used the last of her cash to pay for the bread and cereal. She took Timmy's hand and left the store hoping to have a[n] _____ day of job hunting.

## EXERCISE II—Sentence Completion

*Complete the sentence in a way that shows you understand the meaning of the italicized vocabulary word.*

1. Ralph wanted a *bona fide* New York cheesecake, so he...

2. If you do not wait for *optimum* sailing conditions, you might...

3. The *ambiguous* quote caused controversy because...

4. Sheila, covered in food, *glowered* at the waiter after he...

5. Nathan *impaled* an earthworm on the hook before he...

6. Try not to *deviate* from the subject while you...

7. The formation of a pearl is an *adventitious* effect of...

8. The *fecund* nature of the jungle...

9. Alice thought that she could *edify* her son, but she knew that she could not when...

10. The car salesman *obfuscated* the dissatisfied customer so much that the customer...

11. The uninsured woman *importuned* the hospital to...

12. A *cataclysm* caused by an asteroid striking the earth would probably...

13. The *pedestrian* television program was not worth...

14. You cannot *extenuate* your bad habit of...

15. Martin had a *parochial* fear of travel, so it surprised everyone when he...

## EXERCISE III—Roots, Prefixes, and Suffixes

*Study the entries and answer the questions that follow.*

The root *merge* means "to plunge" or "to immerse."
The root *integr* means "whole," "intact," or "perfect."
The root *lat* means "to carry" or "to bear."
The suffixes *ence* and *ance* mean "the quality of [base]-ing."
The prefix *e* means "out" or "from."
The prefix *co* means "together" or "with."
The prefix *trans* means "across" or "through."

1.  Using literal translations as guidance, define the following words without using a dictionary.

    A.  submerge             D.  integral
    B.  emergence            E.  relate
    C.  merge                F.  collated

2.  The literal meaning of *translate* is _____.

    A person who is carried upward in spirit is said to be _____.

    If someone tells you a story, you can carry it to another person and _____ it to him.

3.  A person with whole character is said to have _____.

    You _____ something by bringing things together as a whole. If you separate the things from the whole, or if you break them up, then you _____ them.

4.  List at least five words that contain the roots *ance* or *ence*.

## EXERCISE IV—Inferences

*Complete the sentences by inferring information about the italicized word from its context.*

1.  Seek a *fecund* area in which to plant the tomatoes and corn if you want to…

2.  People fell asleep during the *pedestrian* film because it was…

3.  The kids went to camp to enjoy the outdoors, but the experience also had the *adventitious* effect of teaching them how to…

# EXERCISE V—Writing

*Here is a writing prompt similar to the one you will find on the writing portion of the SAT.*

Plan and write an essay based on the following statement:

> "... there was one of two things I had a right to, liberty, or death; if I could not have one, I would take de oder; for no man should take me alive; I should fight for my liberty as long as my strength lasted, and when de time came for me to go, de Lord would let dem take me."
>
> –Harriet Tubman

**Assignment:** What do you feel are the two most important things to which people have a right? In an essay, explain the two rights that you feel are most valuable, the importance they have in people's lives, and then speculate how society would change if those rights were taken away. Be certain to support any generalities you make with specific references to the literature you are discussing and to your experience and observation.

**Thesis:** Write a one-sentence response to the above assignment. Make certain this single sentence offers a clear statement of your position.

*Example: Without the rights to both give and receive love, relationships would disintegrate, resulting in a society comprising self-serving people.*

**Organizational Plan:** If your thesis is the point on which you want to end, where does your essay need to begin? List the points of development that are inevitable in leading your reader from your beginning point to your end point. This list is your outline.

**Draft:** Use your thesis as both your beginning and your end. Following your outline, write a good first draft of your essay. Remember to support all your points with examples, facts, references to reading, etc.

**Review and revise:** Exchange essays with a classmate. Using the scoring guide for Development on page 241, score your partner's essay (while he or she scores yours). Focus on the development of ideas and use of language conventions. If necessary, rewrite your essay to improve the development of ideas and/or your use of language.

## Improving Paragraphs

*Read the following passage and then answer the multiple-choice questions that follow. The questions will require you to make decisions regarding the revision of the reading selection.*

1    Sometimes it is nice to marvel at the many products of technology. In a span of fewer than one hundred years, humans have developed antibiotics, space travel, nuclear reactors, digital communications, batteries—oh, wait: we didn't invent batteries. They've been around for quite some time—more than 2,000 years, as a matter of fact.

2    In 1936, workers excavating a 2,000-year-old village near Baghdad find a seemingly unexciting clay pot, roughly six inches tall. The pot, shaped like a small vase, was casually grouped with other artifacts and placed into storage.

3    The clay pot sat untouched for two years, until the day Wilhelm Konig, a German archaeologist, made a close examination of the artifact. To his astonishment, the ancient pot contained a copper cylinder, six inches in length, through which an iron rod hung suspended. An asphalt stopper sealed the cylinder in the pot, and another piece of asphalt beneath the cylinder appeared to serve as an insulator. The iron rod showed signs of corrosion, as though, perhaps, an acidic fluid had been used as an electrolytic solution to establish a current between the copper tube and the iron rod. Doctor Konig had just discovered a 2,000-year-old battery.

4    The battery sparked the imaginations of archaeologists all over the world. How could a civilization that knew nothing about the existence of electricity create a battery? Batteries are expensive even today. More important, why would an ancient civilization *need* a battery?

5    In 1940, well before scientists had finished speculating about the mysterious device, Willard Gray, a scientist at the General Electric High Voltage Laboratory in Massachusetts, decided to conduct an experiment to confirm that the clay pot was indeed a battery. He created a replica of the pot, and, using a copper sulfate solution as an electrolyte, the pot generated one-half volt. The battery was legitimate.

6    The attention of archaeologists was returned to determining the purpose of the battery. Most of the theorists agreed that, based on the findings of silver-plated copper artifacts, the battery was used by the ancients for electroplating, or gilding; however, doubts were instilled about the theory because of the limited potential of the battery.

7    During the 1970s, an Egyptologist built another replica of the battery, but to test this replica, he used an electrolyte that would more likely have been available to the ancients: fresh grape juice. The replica battery reportedly generated nearly one volt. The same researcher allegedly used the replica battery to electroplate a statuette with gold, but any evidence to support the experiment has long vanished. Despite the lack of evidence, scientists still agree that the battery was probably used for plating, or gilding, metal.

8    The Baghdad Battery now sits in the Baghdad Museum with as many as twelve others like it, all dated to the vicinity of 250 B.C. Perhaps if someone had left one sitting out, the world would not have needed to wait for Alessandro Volta to invent the battery—again—in 1799. Who knows what other inventions lie buried beneath the desert sands?

9    Some scientists theorized that the ancients used the batteries for pain relief, because the ancient Greeks were aware that the mysterious quality of electric eels was useful in alleviating aching feet. Others theorize that the batteries were the result of ancient Chinese acupuncture techniques, because electric acupuncture is practiced in modern China. Theories even include shock-inducing, anti-theft devices that ancients might have placed inside statues.

1.   Which of the following corrections would fix an error in paragraph 2?
     A.  Remove the comma after *In 1936*.
     B.  Add *was* before *placed*.
     C.  Change *was casually grouped* to *is casually grouped*.
     D.  Change *shaped like a vase* to *vase-shaped*.
     E.  Change *find* to past tense.

2.   Which of the following sentences should be deleted from paragraph 4?
     A.  sentence 1
     B.  sentence 2
     C.  sentence 3
     D.  sentence 2 and sentence 3
     E.  sentence 1 and sentence 4

3.   Which of the following changes would best improve paragraph 6?
     A.  Add details about the credentials of the theorists.
     B.  Rewrite the paragraph in active voice.
     C.  Include the name of Wilhelm Konig.
     D.  Describe the location of the archeological site where the battery was found.
     E.  Exchange paragraph 2 with paragraph 6.

4.   Which of the following details would best improve the content of the passage without distracting from the topic?
     A.  Briefly explain the concept of electroplating.
     B.  Add another paragraph about Chinese electric acupuncture.
     C.  Add a catchy title.
     D.  Insert a blank space between paragraphs 3 and 4.
     E.  Rewrite the passage to have a tone of skepticism.

5.   Which of the following changes would best improve the conclusion of the passage?
     A.  Rewrite paragraph 9.
     B.  Exchange the first paragraph with the last paragraph.
     C.  Place paragraph 9 to follow paragraph 4.
     D.  Place paragraph 9 to follow paragraph 2.
     E.  Delete paragraph 9.

# Lesson Four

1. **celibate** (sel´ ə bit) *adj.* abstaining from intercourse; unmarried
   In that religion, the priests take vows to remain impoverished and *celibate.*

2. **fortuitous** (fôr tōō´ i təs) *adj.* happening by chance or accident
   My father said meeting my mother was *fortuitous;* my mother said it was fate.
   *syn: accidental; unexpected*　　　　　　　*ant: premeditated; intentional*

3. **recapitulate** (rē kə pich´ ə lāt) *v.* to summarize; to repeat briefly
   Television newsmen always *recapitulate* Presidential news conferences, as if the audience were incapable of understanding what had been said.

4. **perfunctory** (pər fungk´ tə rē) *adj.* done without care; in a routine fashion
   She greeted her guests in a *perfunctory* manner.
   *syn: indifferent; offhand*　　　　　　　*ant: diligent; attentive*

5. **baroque** (bə rōk´) *adj.* overly decorated
   The new dance club had a great light show; the *baroque* furnishings seemed right in place.
   *syn: ornate*　　　　　　　*ant: simple*

6. **hedonism** (hēd´ n iz əm) *n.* pursuit of pleasure, especially of the senses
   John favors *hedonism* over self-sacrifice.

7. **obloquy** (äb´ lə kwē) *n.* strong disapproval; a bad reputation resulting from public criticism
   His behavior brought shame to his family and *obloquy* on himself.
   *syn: censure; rebuke*　　　　　　　*ant: acclaim; praise*

8. **debacle** (dā bä´ kəl) *n.* a complete failure; a total collapse
   After reading the reviews, the actors knew the play was a *debacle* and would close in one night.
   *syn: calamity; catastrophe*　　　　　　　*ant: success; triumph*

9. **quasi-** (kwā´ zī) *adj.* resembling; seeming; half
   Grandfather was only in *quasi*-retirement because he couldn't give up control of the business.

10. **besmirch** (bi smûrch´) *v.* to make dirty; to stain
My ex-best friend tried to *besmirch* my reputation with her vicious gossip.
*syn: soil; sully; smear*          *ant: cleanse*

11. **imperative** (im per´ ə tiv) *adj.* extremely necessary; vitally important
It is *imperative* that you leave immediately.

12. **sacrosanct** (sak´ rō sangkt) *adj.* extremely holy
The detective's orders were to investigate everyone; no person was so *sacrosanct* that he or she was above suspicion.
*syn: divine; angelic*

13. **sadistic** (sə dis´ tik) *adj.* deriving pleasure from inflicting pain on others
Donna took *sadistic* pleasure in tormenting her little sister.
*syn: barbarous; perverse*          *ant: civilized; humane*

14. **demeanor** (di mē´ nər) *n.* behavior; manner of conducting oneself
Believe me, his shy *demeanor* is just an act; he is really quite wild.
*syn: deportment*

15. **facetious** (fə sē´ shəs) *adj.* comical; jocular; flippant
Her *facetious* comments were beginning to get tiresome.
*syn: joking; witty; jocose*          *ant: solemn; serious*

## EXERCISE I—Words in Context

*From the list below, supply the words needed to complete the paragraph. Some words will not be used.*

| | | | |
|---|---|---|---|
| debacle | hedonism | demeanor | quasi- |
| perfunctory | besmirch | obloquy | sadistic |
| imperative | | | |

1.  Advances in technology may have increased our life spans, but they also turned us into a civilization of _____ in which people are slaves to entertainment and self-satisfaction. We no longer question the _____ parenting techniques that produce children with such pathetic _____ that they prefer sitting in living rooms and playing _____ shoot-'em-up video games to going outside and experiencing the most beautiful days of the summer. It is _____ that we nurture and guide the latest generation to appreciate and embrace the beauty of the natural—the real—world. The misconception of children that success in their digital kingdoms is comparable to real, character-inspired success is one of the great _____ of the twenty-first century. Someday, the appropriate _____ will be assigned to parents who allow their own children to become _____zombies whose best talent is playing internet role-playing-games for six hours a night—every night.

*From the list below, supply the words needed to complete the paragraph. Some words will not be used.*

| | | |
|---|---|---|
| hedonism | recapitulate | besmirch |
| baroque | perfunctory | fortuitous |

2.  The _____ interior of Mrs. Adison's house reflected her life of extravagance and world travel. We wandered through the house in amazement, and occasionally we asked Mrs. Adison to _____ the significance of particular items. She told us that some of the items were _____ discoveries that barely survived floods, fires, or revolutions; however, the smoke damage, water stains, and bullet holes that _____ the appearance of the artifacts only added to their intrinsic value.

*From the list below, supply the words needed to complete the paragraph. Some words will not be used.*

**sacrosanct**      **facetious**      **celibate**      **obloquy**      **imperative**

3.    Though four years had passed since Jake Bristol had been declared killed-in-action, his _____ wife, Georgia, refused to date, even at the urging of her family.

"We all loved Jake," said Jake's brother, Robert, "but even the memory of my own brother is not so _____ that you should spend the rest of your life alone." Georgia did not take her eyes off the motionless porch swing.

"Is this a proposal, Bob?" Georgia's _____ reply revealed that she wasn't as depressed as Robert had assumed.

# EXERCISE II—Sentence Completion

*Complete the sentence in a way that shows you understand the meaning of the italicized vocabulary word.*

1.  If you make a *facetious* remark during a job interview, you might...

2.  The congressman experienced *obloquy* as a result of...

3.  Ivan has a bad injury; it is *imperative* that he...

4.  Lori's *demeanor* changed from angry to pleasant when...

5.  No one expected to find such *baroque* furnishings in...

6.  The failing grade *besmirched* Ryan's...

7.  The neighborhood is run down and overgrown, but the *sacrosanct* house of the Jones family is...

8.  Opening the classy restaurant in the small town was a *debacle* because...

9.  People who cannot control their *hedonism* are likely to...

10. New recruits thought the drill sergeant was *sadistic*, but he was actually...

11. Pam blamed the contractors for building the home in a *perfunctory* way when she noticed...

12  In Puritan society, people were expected to remain *celibate* unless...

13. Jerry made a *fortuitous* find when...

14. Please *recapitulate* what you just said, because...

15. Weary of sitting on rocks, the castaway made a *quasi*-recliner from...

## EXERCISE III—Roots, Prefixes, and Suffixes

*Study the entries and answer the questions that follow.*

The root *clin* means "to lean" or "to bend."
The roots *pon* and *pos* mean "to put" or "to place."
The root *hyper* means "excessive."
The root *therm* means "heat."
The prefix *com* means "together."
The prefix *im* means "into."
The prefix *dis* means "apart."
The prefix *de* means "down."

1. Provide literal translations for the following words.

   A   deposit                  D.   dispose
   B.  depose                   E.   compose
   C.  impose                   F.   component

2. If your thoughts lean toward a certain activity, then you have a[n] _____ for that activity.

   If you spend too much time leaning back on the _____, your physical fitness will _____.

3. A[n] _____ child might have trouble sitting still, and a[n] _____ judge might upset the contestants of a singing contest.

4. List all the words that you can think of that contain the root *therm*.

## EXERCISE IV—Inference

*Complete the sentences by inferring information about the italicized word from its context.*

1. Martin asked the speaker to *recapitulate* the last part of the lecture because he...

2. The airline fired the mechanic for his *perfunctory* work after...

3. Hector never had a job, and his belief in *hedonism* was apparent by the way in which he...

## EXERCISE V—Critical Reading

*Below is a pair of reading passages followed by several multiple-choice questions similar to the ones you will encounter on the SAT. Carefully read both passages and choose the best answer to each of the questions.*

*The Love Canal incident, the subject of the following passages, was perhaps the most publicized, though not the worst, environmental catastrophe in United States history. The Love Canal has been a source of controversy for years, specifically in regard to who was responsible for the spread of contamination at the site.*

### Passage 1

At one time, the American dream was simply to own a home. Now, thanks to selfish industrialists, the American dream is to own a home that will not kill the homeowners.

During the 1950s, the Board of Education of Niagara Falls, New York, found the perfect site—so they thought—on which to build a new elementary school. At the center of the 16-acre property southwest of the city was the site known as the Love Canal, a partially completed canal that was dug in the 1890s by William Love, an entrepreneur who sought to use cheap hydroelectric power to run a model industrial city. Love's project failed, and in 1942, Hooker Electrochemical purchased the canal and dumped 20,000 tons of toxic waste in it. Hooker then capped the canal with clay and planted grass on the top. The open field looked like prime real estate to the Board of Education, which needed plenty of land to meet the demands of a rapidly growing population.

Eager to rid itself of a legal dilemma, Hooker Chemical Corporation donated the dump and surrounding area to the school board for $1.00. The School Board paid little notice to the disclaimer on the deed that released Hooker Chemical of any responsibility for future damages caused by buried chemicals; it built two elementary schools, and then sold portions of the property to housing developers.

In the years following the exchange of the Love Canal, the American dream turned into the American nightmare. Chemical vapors wafted through the streets, and strange substances surfaced in the yards. Children who played outside suffered from chemical burns and skin irritations, and residents reported abnormal numbers of miscarriages and birth defects. The families at Love Canal were living in poison.

In the late 1970s, Niagara Falls hired environmental investigators to determine the extent of the Love Canal problem. Teams confirmed the presence of many toxic chemicals in the air and in the ground around the 800 homes and 200 apartments. Black sludge oozed through basement walls, and 55-gallon drums began to surface after heavy rainfalls increased the height of the water table. In 1978, the New York Department of Health declared the Love Canal a health hazard and evacuated the homes closest to the canal. Later that year, President Carter declared the area to be a federal emergency, and another 250 families evacuated the neighborhoods adjacent to the canal. Eventually, 800 families, fearing for their lives, were relocated from their homes near the Love Canal. The homes nearest the canal now lay beneath a clay cap that was constructed in 1984 to contain the millions of gallons of toxins. An eight-foot fence encircles the poisonous field.

In the decade following the initial evacuation of the Love Canal, residents and government agencies filed nearly 1000 lawsuits that totaled over $14 billion. As of 2000, Occidental Chemical, the company that acquired Hooker Chemical, has paid out a paltry $190 million in damages to the government—a fraction of the billions that it generates each year. Such inadequate punitive measures impart only one message to corporations: pollute as much as you want—you can afford it.

## Passage 2

In 1977, when the residents of the Love Canal took to the streets to express rage over living in a former toxic waste dump, many of them blamed the local government—and rightly so. It was the government—bureaucrats enjoying the protection of sovereign immunity—that blatantly ignored the warnings of a chemical company, and then approved the construction of schools and homes on top of a trench full of toxic waste.

The Love Canal, a partially dug canal just southwest of Niagara Falls, New York, was a remnant of a failed turn-of-the-century project to create an advanced industrial city. William Love abandoned the project after running low on funds, and the city of Niagara Falls took ownership of the useless, 3000-foot trench in 1927. In 1942, Hooker Electrochemical identified the sparsely populated, clay-bottomed Love Canal area as a good location to dispose of industrial waste. Hooker purchased the land, and then the company obtained the necessary permits from Niagara Falls to legally dispose of industrial waste in the canal. From 1942 to 1953, Hooker legally buried more than 20,000 tons of industrial waste in barrels. In an age in which no dumping regulations existed, Hooker even took the courteous caution of lining the canal with clay and concrete to prevent leakage. The dump would have met standards that did not even exist until 1980—thirty years after Hooker stopped dumping and capped the canal with four feet of clay.

While Hooker prepared to close the dump in 1953, the Niagara Falls Board of Education was addressing two major problems: booming population and scarce education funds. The school board needed cheap real estate, so when it found the seemingly harmless grassy field that covered the Love Canal, it thought that it had found the perfect spot to build new schools; so perfect, in fact, that it threatened to seize the 16-acre lot through eminent domain in response to the Hooker Corporation's refusal to sell.

Hooker had two options: it could sell the land and retain the ability to warn future developers, or it could allow the city to condemn the Love Canal and thus forfeit the right to prevent future development. Hooker knew that selling a toxic waste dump to vacuous buyers was a legal time bomb, so it tried to take the ethical route of selling the land with special provisions on the deed, notably that the land be used for parks only—no construction. The board, determined to develop the toxic waste dump, rejected the deed. Hooker was forced to simplify the deed until the only remaining provision was a lengthy clause that waived Hooker for any future injuries or deaths caused by the industrial waste. Hooker even went so far as to escort school board officials to the dumpsite to physically see the chemicals for themselves. The board, apparently blind, deaf, and oblivious to the words *injury* and *death* on the deed, approved the contract. Then it started building.

The school board's first inane move was to order the construction of two schools, one of which was directly over the 20,000 tons of poison in the canal. The school ordered thousands of tons of fill to be removed from the top of the canal, and, amazingly, the contractors found chemical pits. Apparently, the school board did not bother telling the contractors that they were working in a vat of hazardous waste. The Board solved the problem by moving the school several feet to avoid the discovered chemicals.

The schools opened by 1957, and the Board of Education sought to sell adjacent land—polluted land—to developers. Hooker Chemical protested the development; it sent representatives to the board meetings to chastise the effort and once again explain that the Love Canal property was unsuitable for any type of construction—especially homes.

Hooker's warnings finally began to sink into the minds of the School Board members, but much to the wrong effect: the board did not want to fix the problem, it just wanted to unload the land and liability faster than before. In the meantime, unfortunately, city workers installed sewer lines in the Love Canal property; the excavation punched holes in the canal walls and the clay cap that contained millions of gallons of toxic sludge.

The Board of Education found developers to buy portions of the Love Canal property, and each new construction further compromised the containment ability of the dumpsite. Chemical fumes seeped into homes, and industrial waste emerged in basements. Children grew sick just playing on their own lawns. In 1978, the President of the United States declared a state of emergency at the Love Canal. In the years that followed, more than 800 families were relocated from the area. Bulldozers razed the homes nearest the canal, and now, a forty-acre clay cap covers the site.

Since 1978, environmental zealots and cause-of-the-week activists have wrongfully depicted Hooker Chemical as a stereotypical evil corporation that profits by intentionally poisoning its patrons; they need to find a different scapegoat, because it is not big industry who fouled up the Love Canal—it was a group of bureaucrats, desperate for cheap land, who ignored repeated warnings that the property was unsuitable for development and *still* demanded possession of it. Ignorance at this level is inexcusable, even for bureaucrats whose poor decisions are not punishable by law.

1.  As used in the second paragraph of passage 1, the word *entrepreneur* most nearly means
    A. millionaire.
    B. attorney.
    C. governor.
    D. industrialist.
    E. visionary.

2.  Which of the following is the best title for passage 1?
    A. Corporate Irresponsibility
    B. Surviving the American Dream
    C. Niagara Falls Down
    D. The Effects of Industrial Waste in Proximity to Residential Neighborhoods
    E. The Results of Inadequate Education Budgets

3.  According to passage 1, Hooker Chemical donated the Love Canal because
    A. it wanted to give back to the community.
    B. school officials were going to seize the land.
    C. it wanted to rid itself of liability for the dump.
    D. it would have looked bad to sell the dump for a profit.
    E. the company experienced layoffs.

4.  According to passage 2, who is responsible for the Love Canal incident?
    A. Hooker Chemical Corporation
    B. the Board of Education
    C. the developers who built homes
    D. the city engineers
    E. the mayor of Niagara Falls

5.  According to passage 2, which is *not* one of the ways that the chemical company tried to warn against developing the Love Canal?
    A. It added special provisions to the original deed to prevent development.
    B. It requested state intervention when the school tried to take the land.
    C. It sent representatives to board meetings.
    D. It initially refused to sell the Love Canal site.
    E. It brought school officials to the site to see the chemicals.

6. As used in the eighth paragraph of passage 2, the word *razed* most nearly means
   A. burned.
   B. flattened.
   C. buried.
   D. remodeled.
   E. sold.

7. Which of the following is the best title for passage 2?
   A. Digging for the Truth About Toxic Waste
   B. Recovering Former Dumps
   C. Occidental's Accident
   D. Bureaucratic Failures
   E. Passing the Buck

8. Which of the following best describes the tone of both passages?
   A. Passage 1 is celebrative, and passage 2 is solemn.
   B. Both passages portray a tone of indifference to the subject.
   C. Passage 2 contains more supporting data than passage 1.
   D. Both passages have a cynical tone.
   E. Passage 1 is fictional, while passage 2 is factual.

9. Which of the following best describes a conflict of supporting information between the two passages?
   A. Passage 1 claims that the company donated the land, while passage 2 claims that the company sold the land.
   B. Passage 1 suggests that the company dumped 20,000 tons of waste in the canal, while passage 2 suggests that the company dumped 20,000 gallons of waste in the canal.
   C. According to passage 2, no homes around the Love Canal were bull-dozed.
   D. Hooker Chemical constructed a clay cap over the canal before selling it.
   E. Passage 2 claims that the Niagara River was contaminated, but passage 1 suggests that the river was not contaminated.

10. The authors of both passages would probably agree that
   A. multiple agencies were responsible for the Love Canal incident.
   B. Hooker Chemical should not have donated the Love Canal.
   C. the Occidental Corporation should not have permitted development.
   D. the Niagara Falls Board of Education lacked adequate funds.
   E. Niagara Falls should have listened to the chemical company.

# Lesson Five

1. **fop** (fop)  *n.*  an excessively fashion-conscious man
When he came in wearing a bow tie, a diamond pinky ring, and carrying a pearl-handled cane, we knew he was a *fop*.
*syn: dandy*

2. **imprecation** (im pri kā´ shən)  *n.*  a curse
Jennifer was so angry she pronounced an *imprecation* on him, his family, and all his friends.
*syn: condemnation; anathema*          *ant: blessing*

3. **non sequitur** (non sek´ wi tər)  *n.*  something that does not logically follow
"That he would not be a good mayor because he can't control his own family is a *non sequitur*," said John.
*syn: fallacy; misconception*

4. **sanguine** (sang´ gwin)  *adj.*  cheerful; optimistic
Sally's *sanguine* personality made everyone in her company pleased to be with her.

5. **bowdlerize** (bōd´ ler īz)  *v.*  to remove offensive passages of a play, novel, etc.
If the editors *bowdlerize* much more of the book, there won't be anything left to read.
*syn: censor*

6. **impair** (im pâr´)  *v.*  to weaken; to cause to become worse
Mother used to say that reading in poor light could *impair* your vision.
*syn: damage; deteriorate*          *ant: enhance*

7. **panegyric** (pan ə jir´ ik)  *n.*  an expression of praise
The ancient Greeks gave *panegyrics* and crowns of ivy in tribute to their heroes.
*syn: tribute; extolment*          *ant: denunciation*

8. **quandary** (kwon´ drē)  *n.*  a puzzling situation; a dilemma
John was in a *quandary* deciding what his major should be.
*syn: predicament*

9. **ebullient** (i bŏŏl´ yənt)  *adj.*  enthusiastic
The *ebullient* crowd cheered as the royal family appeared.
*syn: exuberant; lively*          *ant: dejected; dispirited*

10. **deference** (def´ ər əns)  *n.*  respect; consideration
In *deference* to the young widow, we moved quietly aside and allowed her to leave first.

11. **carnal** (kär´ nəl)  *adj.*  relating to physical appetite, especially sexual
After receiving complaints, the town council decided to remove the *carnal* statue from the park area.
*syn: erotic*                                        *ant: chaste; modest*

12. **nebulous** (neb´ yə ləs)  *adj.*  hazy; vague; uncertain
He had a *nebulous* feeling of fear all day, but he didn't understand why until the thunder started.
*syn: cloudy; indistinct; obscure*                   *ant: distinct; precise*

13. **rakish** (rā´ kish)  *adj.*  dashingly stylish and confident
Wanting to look *rakish* for his job interview, Jeremy shined his shoes and pressed razor-edge creases into his shirt and slacks.
*syn: dapper; jaunty*                                *ant: slovenly; disheveled*

14. **elegy** (el´ ə jē)  *n.*  a sad or mournful poem
The reading of the *elegy* brought tears during the funeral.
*syn: dirge; lament*

15. **pedantic** (pə dan´ tik)  *adj.*  tending to show off one's learning
After one year of college, Tom lost all of his friends because of his *pedantic* behavior.
*syn: bookish*

## EXERCISE I—Words in Context

*From the list below, supply the words needed to complete the paragraph. Some words will not be used.*

| | | | |
|---|---|---|---|
| nebulous | imprecation | pedantic | deference |
| impair | fop | rakish | carnal |

1.  Martin, a[n] _____ since high school, had at least nine pairs of sneakers in his closet. The _____ man wouldn't even go to the gym if he weren't wearing crisp new workout clothes. His habit of looking in every mirror he passed in public had alienated him from his friends, and when he returned to Uniontown after earning his doctorate, his _____ conduct drove his family away. Martin never realized that his vanity _____ his social life; his _____ explanations never included any faults of his own. He reasoned that his good looks and superior intellect were _____ that he would just have to live with.

*From the list below, supply the words needed to complete the paragraph. Some words will not be used.*

| | | | |
|---|---|---|---|
| **sanguine** | **ebullient** | **elegy** | **fop** |
| **panegyric** | **non sequitur** | **deference** | |

2.  All the citizens of the small town attended the viewing to show their
    _____ for the late Dr. Clarke. A local writer read a[n] _____
    that recalled Dr. Clarke's friendly, _____ attitude and _____
    approach to caring for the townspeople. He had known all of his patients
    by their first names, and he had made house calls at no additional expense.
    The children of the town remembered Dr. Clarke not only as their gentle
    doctor, but also as the man who occasionally stood on the bleachers dur-
    ing soccer matches to shout a[n] _____ for the little town's home
    team.

*From the list below, supply the words needed to complete the paragraph. Some words will not be used.*

| | | |
|---|---|---|
| **carnal** | **bowdlerize** | **non sequitur** |
| **quandary** | **pedantic** | |

3.  Many of the world's greatest works of literature and drama contain vio-
    lent or _____ contexts, and some groups regularly attempt to
    _____ the works until there is scarcely a book left to read. Whether
    people, specifically school-aged children, should be allowed to read such
    literature has been a[n] _____ of parents and educators for decades.
    Some people claim that exposure to immoral texts will have negative
    effects on young readers; however, others feel that the idea of children suf-
    fering as a result of reading books is a[n] _____.

## EXERCISE II—Sentence Completion

*Complete the sentence in a way that shows you understand the meaning of the italicized vocabulary word.*

1. When Dawn recited the moving *elegy* during the funeral, some of the guests…

2. Censors often *bowdlerize* novels because…

3. Finding a diamond bracelet in the parking lot created a *quandary* for Gary, because he…

4. The crowd screamed *panegyrics* when…

5. The *pedantic* teacher offered to chaperone the field trip, but the students…

6. Out of *deference* for the fallen soldier, the honor guard…

7. The *rakish* young professional stood out among…

8. Some actors are regarded as *fops* because they…

9. The coach maintained a *sanguine* attitude even though…

10. Dave's *ebullient* interest in math led him to…

11. Superstitions are silly; to have bad luck is a *non sequitur* to…

12. The old hermit put an *imprecation* on the entire family because…

13. When the teacher sees your *nebulous* essay on the test, she will know that…

14. You will probably *impair* your hearing if you…

15. The piranhas went into a *carnal* frenzy when…

## EXERCISE III—Roots, Prefixes, and Suffixes

*Study the entries and answer the questions that follow.*

The root *petr* means "stone."
The root *sist* means "to stand," "to stop," or "to set."
The suffix *ous* means "full of."
The roots *viv* and *vit* mean "to live."
The root *glyph* means "to carve."
The suffix *sub* means "under."
The suffix *id* means "tending to."
The suffix *al* means "pertaining to."

1. Provide literal translations for the following words.

   A. vivid           D. revitalize
   B. vivacious       E. exist
   C. vital           F. insist

2. Someone or something that has been turned to stone is _____. A[n] _____ would be a good place to find *petroglyphs*, and it would also be a good place to practice *petrology*, which is the study of _____.

3. *Subsist* literally translates to "stand under." Explain how *subsist*, which means "to maintain life," evolved from "stand under."

4. We use the term _____ to describe oils that we extract from the earth to use as fuel.

5. List as many words as you can think of that end with the suffix *id*.

## EXERCISE IV—Inference

*Complete the sentences by inferring information about the italicized word from its context.*

1. Frank called the stylish bachelor a *fop* because the man usually spent...

2. The career criminal had no *deference* for...

3. If Luke is not *ebullient* about helping you fix the car, then you should...

## EXERCISE V—Writing

*Here is a writing prompt similar to the one you will find on the writing portion of the SAT.*

Plan and write an essay based on the following statement:

> American culture positively recognizes single mother-hood, while debasing single fatherhood because men do not have a positive identity as fathers outside marriage. Therefore, women often possess a certain advantage over men, creating what Barbara Dafoe Whitehead calls a "fatherhood problem." Women provide emotional ties between fathers and children, and without women and marriage, men must overcome substantial obstacles in eliminating the negative stereotype associated with unmarried fathers.

**Assignment**: Write an essay in which you support or refute Barbara Whitehead's assertion. Be certain to support your point with evidence and examples from literature, current events, or your own personal experience or observation.

**Thesis**: Write a one-sentence response to the above assignment. Make certain this single sentence offers a clear statement of your position.

*Example: Single fathers can be positive influences and nurturing caregivers to children, but they do not have any more obstacles to overcome than single mothers, who must endure lower than average wages and long-standing stereo-types.*

**Organizational Plan**: If your thesis is the point on which you want to end, where does your essay need to begin? List the points of development that are inevitable in leading your reader from your beginning point to your end point. This list is your outline.

**Draft**: Use your thesis as both your beginning and your end. Following your outline, write a good first draft of your essay. Remember to support all your points with examples, facts, references to reading, etc.

**Review and revise**: Exchange essays with a classmate. Using the scoring guide for Sentence Formation and Variety on page 242, score your partner's essay (while he or she scores yours). Focus on sentence structure and the use of language conventions. If necessary, rewrite your essay to improve the sentence structure and/or your use of language.

## Identifying Sentence Errors

*Identify the grammatical error in each of the following sentences. If the sentence contains no error, select answer choice E.*

1. Five years,  three of which Shelia was out of the country, were a long time
     (A)         (B)               (C)                        (D)
   to wait.    No error
                 (E)

2. Sammy Sosa's use of a corked bat destroyed many young athletes'
       (A)                       (B)
   allusions about the popular baseball hero.    No error
     (C)                         (D)     (E)

3. During track season,  Samantha and my statistics are usually identical.
                 (A)     (B)    (C)         (D)
   No error
   (E)

4. The club encouraged many women in the community to join, including
                                  (A)      (B)
   Patricia and myself,  even though we had only recently moved to town.
          (C)         (D)
   No error
   (E)

5. To make cookies, blend two sticks of margarine with the vanilla and sugar
      (A)                             (B)
   until the sugar has dissolved.        No error
   (C)           (D)              (E)

## Improving Sentences

*The underlined portion of each sentence below contains some flaw. Select the answer choice that best corrects the flaw.*

6.  At home during the summer, young adults are scrutinized <u>by their parents, at college they are</u> given the opportunity to make their own decisions.
    A.  by their parents, but at college they are
    B.  by their parents: while at college they are
    C.  by their parents; but, at college they are
    D.  by his or her parents, at college they are
    E.  by their parents, at college he or she is

7.  Having read the contract, <u>a blue pen was used at the bottom by Yvonne to sign her name.</u>
    A.  Yvonne used at the bottom to sign her name, a blue pen.
    B.  at the bottom, Yvonne used a blue pen to sign her name.
    C.  a blue pen was used by Yvonne to sign her name at the bottom.
    D.  Yvonne used a blue pen to sign her name at the bottom.
    E.  a blue pen used by Yvonne to sign her name was at the bottom.

8.  My favorite high school teacher <u>is not only president of the local National Education Association but also of the Illinois Association of Teachers of English.</u>
    A.  is the local National Education Association president but also the Illinois Association of Teachers of English president.
    B.  is president of the local National Education Association but also of the Illinois Association of Teachers of English.
    C.  is not only president of the National Education Association and also the Illinois Association of Teachers of English.
    D.  is president of the National Education Association but also of the Illinois Association of Teachers of English.
    E.  is president not only of the National Education Association but also of the Illinois Association of Teachers of English.

9. <u>I am taking graduate classes this summer, and I will be better qualified to teach collegiate-level courses this fall.</u>
    A. I am taking graduate classes this summer, so I will be better qualified to teach collegiate-level courses this fall.
    B. This summer I am taking graduate classes, and I will be better qualified to teach collegiate-level courses this fall.
    C. I am taking graduate classes this summer, but I will be better qualified to teach collegiate-level courses this fall.
    D. Teaching collegiate-level courses this fall means that I must take graduate courses this summer.
    E. To be better qualified to teach collegiate-level courses this fall I must take graduate courses this summer.

10. <u>Having promised to be home after work, Mrs. Thompson was irritated when her husband came in at nine o'clock.</u>
    A. Mrs. Thompson was irritated, having promised to be home after work, when her husband came in at nine o'clock.
    B. Mrs. Thompson was irritated when her husband, having promised to be home after work, came in at nine o'clock .
    C. Having promised to be home after work, Mrs. Thompson was irritated by her husband when he came in at nine o'clock.
    D. Coming in at nine o'clock, Mrs. Thompson was irritated by her husband who promised to be home after work.
    E. Mrs. Thompson was irritated when her husband, having promised to come home after work, came in at nine o'clock.

# Lesson Six

1. **antipathy** (an tip´ ə thē) *n.* an intense dislike
   So great was her feeling of *antipathy* that she was afraid that it showed in her face.
   *syn: aversion*                    *ant: affinity*

2. **elucidate** (i lōō´ si dāt) *v.* to make clear
   To *elucidate* his theory, he drew a large diagram on the board.
   *syn: explain; clarify*              *ant: obscure*

3. **imminent** (im´ ə nənt) *adj.* likely to happen; threatening
   Though the danger was *imminent,* the crew seemed quite relaxed.
   *syn: impending; approaching*        *ant: distant; delayed*

4. **banal** (bā´ nəl) *adj.* common, ordinary
   His *banal* remarks quickly bored the entire class.
   *syn: trivial; insipid*              *ant: original; fresh*

5. **obdurate** (äb´ də rət) *adj.* stubborn; hardhearted
   The young boy was *obdurate* in his refusal to make any trade.
   *syn: inflexible; obstinate*         *ant: compliant; amenable*

6. **peruse** (pə rōōz´) *v.* to read carefully; scrutinize
   Bob *peruses* the classified ads every day to try to find a part-time job.

7. **bedlam** (bed´ ləm) *n.* a noisy uproar; a scene of wild confusion
   The concert hall was sheer *bedlam* until the rock star appeared.
   *syn: mayhem; chaos*

8. **affluence** (af´ lōō əns) *n.* wealth; richness
   Paul earned his fortune without relying on the *affluence* of his family.
   *syn: fortune*

9. **scurrilous** (skûr´ ə ləs) *adj.* coarsely abusive; vulgar
   The *scurrilous* patrons of the saloon were often seen shouting and fighting.
   *syn: indecent*                    *ant: respectable*

10. **parody** (par´ ə dē) *n.* a work which imitates another in a ridiculous manner
    Joan's *parody* of the English teacher was funny to everyone but the English teacher.
    *syn: caricature; burlesque; lampoon*

11. **sedulous** ( sej´ ə ləs) *adj.* hard working; diligent
Everyone knew Jason would get ahead in the world because he was *sedulous* in all he undertook.
*syn: studious; assiduous*            *ant: lazy; lax*

12. **onerous** (ōn´ er əs) *adj.* burdensome; heavy; hard to endure
The doctor had the *onerous* job of informing the family of the child's death.
*syn: crushing; distressing*

13. **amoral** (ā môr´ əl) *adj.* lacking a sense of right and wrong
The *amoral* henchmen obeyed all of the boss's orders, no matter how despicable.
*syn: corrupt; evil*           *ant: innocent; virtuous*

14. **eschew** (es chōō´) *v.* to keep away from; to avoid; to shun
The minister advised the congregation to *eschew* temptation.
          *ant: embrace; welcome*

15. **denouement** (dā nōō män´) *n.* an outcome; result
The novel would have been exciting if it were not for the boring *denouement*.
*syn: conclusion*

## EXERCISE I—Words in Context

*From the list below, supply the words needed to complete the paragraph. Some words will not be used.*

| | | | |
|---|---|---|---|
| bedlam | scurrilous | amoral | elucidate |
| banal | eschew | obdurate | imminent |

1.     Saturday had been a[n] _____, uneventful day until the special report interrupted every television and radio broadcast in the city. A news anchorman _____ the _____ threat of an approaching tidal wave, and, in minutes, the coastal city erupted into _____. According to the experts, the 120-foot tidal wave would obliterate the city in forty minutes—not nearly enough time for an organized evacuation of three million people.

The panic turned humans into _____ animals. In the rush to escape to the high ground beyond the peninsula, people who were once pleasant and mannerly now screamed _____ remarks at anyone preventing their fast escape. Ordinary people who had no means of transportation carjacked automobiles and threw the operators to the ground. Mobs fleeing apartment buildings trampled anyone not fast enough to keep up. There were also thousands of people who were too _____ to believe the alerts; they stayed in their homes and made futile preparations.

*From the list below, supply the words needed to complete the paragraph. Some words will not be used.*

**onerous     bedlam     eschew     sedulous     affluence     peruse**

2.     Kim was a[n] _____ office manager with an impeccable record, but none of her experiences prepared her for the _____ task of firing Bill. Before the meeting, she _____ Bill's file to learn where his productivity declined. Bill was well-liked in the office, so Kim knew that Bill's coworkers would probably _____ her for firing their friend.

*From the list below, supply the words needed to complete the paragraph. Some words will not be used.*

**scurrilous          parody          affluence**
**antipathy          elucidate          denouement**

3.     The show that we watched last night was actually a[n] _____ of a popular Shakespeare play; all the major characters were animals, and it was a comedy rather than a tragedy, unlike the original play. The plot essentially remained the same: a prince of great _____ is the target of his evil stepbrother's _____. The _____ of the new play is different because at the end of the play, the prince forgives his stepbrother instead of fighting him to the death.

## EXERCISE II—Sentence Completion

*Complete the sentence in a way that shows you understand the meaning of the italicized vocabulary word.*

1. Be sure to *peruse* the contract before you...

2. While driving in the car, dad has the habit of singing *parodies* for every song he...

3. The *amoral* prisoner never showed...

4. If you *elucidate* your point well enough, your listeners will...

5. The *antipathy* between the opposing teams was obvious during...

6. Due to the *imminent* snowstorm, classes tomorrow will...

7. Most of the novel is entertaining, but the *denouement* is...

8. Casey decided to change her *banal,* daily routine by...

9. The musician was once a popular figure of *affluence*, but now she...

10. The judge warned Veronica to curb her *scurrilous* language or she would be...

11. Ken liked the money, but he hated his *onerous* job of...

12. The stadium exploded into *bedlam* when the referee...

13. Air travel is statistically safer than automobile travel, but my *obdurate* friend still...

14. In accordance with its customs, the Puritan community *eschewed* the man who...

15. The job would normally take a week to complete, but Roger is a *sedulous* worker who can...

## EXERCISE III—Roots, Prefixes, and Suffixes

*Study the entries and answer the questions that follow.*

The root *pel* means "to push" or "to drive."
The roots *sum* and *sumpt* mean "take."
The root *celer* means "swift."
The prefix *con* means "with" or "together."
The prefix *dis* means "apart" or "in different directions."
The prefix *ex* means "out" or "from."
The suffix *ator* means "one who does."
The suffix *ion* means "the act of."

1.  Using literal translations as guidance, define the following words without using a dictionary.

    A.  expel
    B.  dispel
    C.  propeller
    D.  consumption
    E.  sumptuous
    F.  accelerator

2.  Someone who moves with *celerity* is moving _____.
    The word *accelerate* means _____, but if you slow down, you _____.

3.  You create a[n] _____ by taking excerpts from your career history and writing them down; however, do not _____ that someone will hire you without an interview.

4.  If you drive something forward, you _____ it, but if you drive something back, you _____ it.

    A salesperson might _____ you to purchase a product, but a threat to your safety would _____ you to take cover. You will then need to _____ rumors that you ran away.

5.  List as many words as you can think of that begin with the prefix *con*.

6.  List as many words as you can think of that contain the suffix *ator*.

## EXERCISE IV—Inference

*Complete the sentences by inferring information about the italicized word from its context.*

1.  Tyler was accustomed to *onerous* labor, so the task of...

2.  The jury could not make a deliberation because one *obdurate* juror refused to...

3.  Dr. Bach *elucidates* his diagnoses for patients so that they can...

## EXERCISE V—Critical Reading

*Below is a reading passage followed by several multiple-choice questions similar to the ones you will encounter on the SAT. Carefully read the passage and choose the best answer for each of the questions.*

*The author of the following passage describes the evolution of American handwriting and comments about the decline of the art.*

The spoken word, no matter how fierce, quickly dissipates; certainly, even the finest words are at the mercy of memory. When memories die, not even the greatest speeches and stories in history can be saved. The only way to ensure the continued existence of such thought is to bond it to a medium more permanent than
5   the fickle mind—a medium that will live ages beyond the purveyor: paper. Whether the thought is the next Magna Carta, Declaration of Independence, or a simple grocery list, it will become an artifact that archaeologists will pore over for days when they discover it beneath a scrap of plastic, fifty feet below the surface of the earth, two thousand years from today. For all you know, that little scrap featuring your
10  penmanship—your psychological profile, essentially—will be the only relic of a lost art in the eon following the Age of Information. Think about it the next time you haphazardly scribble a note using a jumble of cursive and printed letters; is that how you really want to represent yourself to your future progeny?
     The Roman Empire recognized the importance of excellent penmanship, as can
15  be observed by the Latin carved into the many stone remnants of Roman civilization. Their simple alphabet is still the foundation of the western world's modern alphabet, but in the centuries after the fall of the Romans, the way in which letters were written varied among European cultures. As a general change, lower case letters were added to the Roman alphabet; however, specific, stylistic changes differed
20  from region to region.

During the Dark Ages after the fall of the Roman Empire, little thought was given to good handwriting; however, little thought was given to literacy at all. Writing supplies, especially paper, were rare, expensive, and reserved for the most important documents and people.

25 Around the middle of the seventh century, the art of writing experienced brief standardization during the Carolingian Period, but writing soon regressed to the various gothic calligraphies that characterize medieval documents. The printing was, and is still, doubtlessly beautiful; however, the penmanship that we now regard as fine art was too tedious to standardize among the largely illiterate mass-
30 es.

As commerce flourished and governments developed, so did the need for a swift method of writing. The cursive handwriting that we know today, despite its woeful decline, originated in the Renaissance, when writers discarded ornate, gothic print for expedient, connected script. Script letters, unlike printed letters, were designed
35 specifically to connect. Prior to script, penmen had to attach handwritten letters with lines in an additional step. The Elizabethan hand, observable in William Shakespeare's sixteenth-century writings, combined elements of gothic print with script. The new, convenient script quickly spread throughout Europe, but the invention of the printing press temporarily stifled efforts to standardize a particular
40 hand.

In the Victorian Era, a time famous for artful precision and detail, the world identified the need for clean, standardized handwriting. Enough time had passed for the Elizabethan script to evolve into copperplate, which is the roundhand forerunner of the cursive taught today. In 1848, Platt Rogers Spencer published the technique
45 for a very refined form of roundhand script, and it became the model for American penmanship for more than 100 years. The beautiful Spencerian script augmented the beauty of the Victorian Age and made even the most mundane documents— property deeds, shipping manifests, professional certifications—cherished works of art worthy of framing. Such fine writing reflects the conscience of the nation's ear-
50 lier denizens; they lived in an era in which pride, precision, and beauty were integral parts of daily living. Businessmen spent considerable time practicing their handwriting, for certainly no one would take them seriously if they produced sloppy, illegible documents.

Near the late nineteenth century, a teacher and master penman named Austin
55 Palmer noticed a need for a less demanding penmanship for business handwriting. Businesses had limited time to produce large amounts of writing, and, despite the existence of a Spencerian business hand devoid of flourishes and bold letters, the arm movements required for the font exhausted writers. Palmer simplified the Spencerian script, and, by 1912, over one million copies of the Palmer Method text-
60 book had been sold. Many schools continued to teach the intricate Spencerian script until the middle of the century, but eventually, the practical Palmer style, assisted by the inventions of typewriters and copiers, rendered the Spencerian hand obsolete.

Computers, email, and other digital forms of communication are proliferating
65 exponentially. Many people, satisfied with the monotony of mass-produced greeting cards, mini-malls, and frozen-yogurt shops, expect penmanship to go the way of candlemaking, and they might be right. The eloquent script of yesteryear, like classic automobiles and awe-inspiring architecture, is dying. Style and grace are not

intrinsic to modern life; elements that serve only to impress or to inspire—are not
70  cost effective. Soon, no one will remember the era in which people, in order to con-
vey their feelings, actually sat down and used their primitive hands to write letters
on paper. It's probably for the better; after all, why would someone want to sign a
letter by hand if he or she has an email signature block as personal and sentimental as *DAvM0272@electomail.com?*

1.  As used in line 13, *progeny* most nearly means
    A.  ancestors.
    B.  predecessors.
    C.  family geniuses.
    D.  sisters and brothers.
    E.  descendants.

2.  The purpose of the first paragraph is to
    A.  express the importance of penmanship.
    B.  debunk myths about desktop publishing.
    C.  explain how fine writing is disappearing.
    D.  inform about the phases of handwriting.
    E.  persuade people to surrender their pens.

3.  As used in line 50, *denizens* most nearly means
    A.  relatives.
    B.  commanders.
    C.  dwellers.
    D.  totalitarians.
    E.  professionals.

4.  Which answer best describes the implication of the following
    sentence (lines 49-51)?

    > Such fine writing reflects the conscience of the nation's earlier
    > denizens; they lived in an era in which pride, precision, and
    > beauty were integral parts of daily living.

    A.  Queen Victorian was a strict taskmaster.
    B.  People in the author's time forego pride, precision, and beauty.
    C.  Victorian people were very superficial.
    D.  Victorian people had vivid dreams of success.
    E.  Pride, precision, and beauty are mandatory elements of penmanship.

5. As used in line 62, the word *hand* most nearly means
   A. appendage.
   B. style.
   C. pen.
   D. drawing.
   E. assistance.

6. Austin Palmer created a new method of writing because
   A. he and Spencer had a professional rivalry.
   B. the Department of Education requested a simple style of writing.
   C. Spencerian writing was hard to reproduce on typewriters.
   D. schools and businesses experienced paper shortages.
   E. the Spencerian method was tiring for writers.

7. As used in line 69, *intrinsic* most nearly means
   A. avoided.
   B. inherent.
   C. substituted.
   D. popular.
   E. sentimental.

8. The last line of the passage can be most accurately described as an example of
   A. opinion.
   B. personification.
   C. iambic pentameter.
   D. irony.
   E. metaphor.

9. According to the passage, which of the following choices is *not* a phase in the evolution of penmanship?
   A. the development of Edwardian italic writing
   B. America adopting the Spencerian writing method
   C. standardization during the Carolingian Period
   D. changes to the Roman alphabet
   E. the introduction of the Palmer method

10. This passage would probably be found in a[n]
    A. department store catalog.
    B. arts and crafts book.
    C. medical journal.
    D. newspaper column.
    E. art history book.

# Lesson Seven

1.  **adroit**  (ə droit´)  *adj.*  skillful; clever
    He was not an *adroit* speaker, but he was a genius with numbers.
    *syn: dexterous; apt*                          *ant: clumsy; awkward*

2.  **macroscopic**  (mak rə skop´ ik)  *adj.*  visible to the naked eye
    On a clear night, the Milky Way appears *macroscopic*.
                                              *ant: microscopic*

3.  **fatuous**  (fach´ ōō əs)  *adj.* foolish; inane
    Her *fatuous* simpering began to grate on our nerves.
    *syn: silly*                          *ant: sensible; wise*

4.  **bovine**  (bō´ vīn)  *adj.*  pertaining to cows or cattle
    The large animal figures in the cave drawing depicted *bovine* creatures.

5.  **ferret**  (fer´ it)  *v.*  to search or drive out
    John knew the answer was in the text, but he just couldn't *ferret* it out.

6.  **affectation**  (af ek tā´ shən)  *n.*  a phony attitude; pose
    Ginger could not stand the *affectations* of the girls in the fashion clique.
    *syn: insincerity; sham*                 *ant: sincerity; genuineness*

7.  **knell**  (nel)  *n.*  a sound made by a bell, often rung slowly for a death or funeral
    The *knell* of the church bell told the town that Gertrude had passed away.

8.  **dichotomy**  (dī kot´ ə mē)  *n.*  a division into two parts
    Disagreements among board members created a *dichotomy* of the charitable organizations.

9.  **callow**  (kal´ ō)  *adj.*  young and inexperienced
    The *callow* boy left for the war, but an exhausted man returned.
    *syn: immature*                          *ant: mature; sophisticated*

10. **laconic**  (la kon´ ik)  *adj.*  using few words; short; concise
    He was a *laconic* man who wasted few words.
    *syn: pithy; taciturn*                    *ant: verbose; loquacious*

11. **quiddity**  (kwid´ i tē)  *n.*  an essential quality
    Patience is the *quiddity* of a good teacher.
    *syn: essence*

12. **patent** (pat´ nt) *adj.* evident or obvious
When the electronics store saw the *patent* abuse of the game system, they refused to grant a refund.
*syn: indisputable; apparent*

13. **peccadillo** (pek ə dil´ ō) *n.* a minor offense; a misdeed
Stealing tips from tables was a *peccadillo* in Bill's mind, but a major offense in the minds of the waiters.

14. **sagacious** (sə gā´ shəs) *adj.* wise; having keen perception and sound judgment
The *sagacious* old man always had the answers to moral problems.
*syn: shrewd; intelligent*                    *ant: obtuse; fatuous*

15. **rationalize** (rash´ ə nə līz) *v.* to make an excuse for
The boy tried to *rationalize* his absence from school.
*syn: justify*

## EXERCISE I—Words in Context

*From the list below, supply the words needed to complete the paragraph. Some words will not be used.*

| | | |
|---|---|---|
| macroscopic | adroit | dichotomy |
| patent | quiddity | laconic |

1.  The inventor's presentation of the new microprocessor was a[n] _____ of theory and application, and his _____ explanations were easy to understand. During the description of the chip's _____ components, the inventor said that the _____ of the new design was its amazing speed; the processor was over 1,000 times faster than any previous design.

*From the list below, supply the words needed to complete the paragraph. Some words will not be used.*

| | | | |
|---|---|---|---|
| dichotomy | sagacious | knell | affectation |
| bovine | patent | fatuous | |

2.    The cows in the _____ pasture were marked for slaughter, and the occasional clanking cowbell reminded Dana of death _____ from a church bell. Her brother died three months ago, and any metal-on-metal sound made Dana recall the broken silence on the morning of the funeral. While at work, Dana maintained the _____ that she was fine, but her family had no trouble detecting her _____ depression. As her _____ father pointed out to the rest of the family, Dana had the closest relationship with her older brother, and she would need more time to mourn.

*From the list below, supply the words needed to complete the paragraph. Some words will not be used.*

| | | | |
|---|---|---|---|
| rationalize | quiddity | callow | adroit |
| ferret | fatuous | peccadillo | macroscopic |

3.    Before getting fired from his warehouse job and being arrested for grand theft, Eric _____ his criminal actions as _____ that were not really hurting anyone. The _____ thief had the _____ notion that no one would notice that $17,000.00 in merchandise simply had vanished. In a successful effort to _____ out the thief, the _____ warehouse manager conducted secret inventories every day for two weeks.

## EXERCISE II—Sentence Completion

*Complete the sentence in a way that shows you understand the meaning of the italicized vocabulary word.*

1. The *knelling* bells summoned…

2. Don't *rationalize* your actions; you had no reason to…

3. The *laconic* soldier guarding the gate would not…

4. The *adroit* mechanic repaired the biplane even though he…

5. To Susan, stealing office supplies is a *peccadillo*, but to the manager…

6. The defamed actor said the accusation was a *patent* lie that was meant to…

7. The three boys did not cease their *fatuous* behavior, so the teacher…

8. Exercise is a *quiddity* of…

9. At the crime scene, look for *macroscopic* evidence before you…

10. The Bundy family put on an *affectation* of wealth, but everyone knew…

11. The *callow* boy wanted to hike the Appalachian trail now, but his parents told him…

12. It took three weeks to drive the *bovine* herd…

13. The *sagacious* oracle warned the Viking warriors…

14. The sergeant ordered Corporal Duncan to enter the cave and *ferret* out…

15. The *adroit* thief eluded capture by…

## EXERCISE III—Roots, Prefixes, and Suffixes

*Study the entries and answer the questions that follow.*

The root *tach* means "swift" or "speed."
The roots *mid*, *med*, and *meso* mean "middle."
The root *bol* means "to throw" or "to put."
The roots *prov* and *prob* mean "good" or "to test."
The prefix *meta* means "changed."
The suffix *meter* means "measure."
The prefix *inter* means "among."
The prefixes *em* and *im* mean "in."
The prefix *sym* means "with" or "together."
The prefix *hyper* means "excessive."

1.  Using literal translations as guidance, define the following words without using a dictionary.

    A.  prove              D.  median
    B.  disapprove         E.  metabolism
    C.  Mesoamerica        F.  improve

2.  A tachometer _____ the _____ at which an engine runs.

3.  A[n] _____ meal is neither bad nor good—it is simply in the middle.

    Athletes who have better skills than beginners but fewer skills than experts are often described as being _____, or "among the middle."

4.  An obstruction in a blood vessel is called a[n] _____, but if you exaggerate, or throw the meaning of something too far, then you have used a[n] _____.

    A skull and crossbones on a black flag could mean anything by itself, but if you see the flag flying above a ship, you might throw its meaning together with what it represents and realize that the design is a[n] _____ of piracy.

5.  The Mars satellite will _____ the composition of the planet's surface. If someone has good chances of winning, then that person will _____ win.

## EXERCISE IV—Inference

*Complete the sentences by inferring information about the italicized word from its context.*

1. The captors imprisoned Agent Sparks in a steel cage, but they also posted guards around it because the *adroit* prisoner...

2. Captain Jack, now a prisoner on his own ship, wished he had listened to the *sagacious* first mate's warning that...

3. Janice's *affectations* included speaking in a phony British accent and...

## EXERCISE V—Writing

*Here is a writing prompt similar to the one you will find on the writing portion of the SAT.*

Plan and write an essay on the following statement:

> American essayist and philosopher Ralph Waldo Emerson wrote: "A friend is Janus-faced;[1] he looks to the past and the future. He is a child of all my foregoing hours, the prophet of those to come."
>
> Someone who has been that kind of friend to me is...

[1]Janus is the Roman god of entrances and exits of life. He is pictured with two faces, one facing forward, the other behind. The month of January is named after him.

**Assignment:** Write an essay in which you discuss how the person you have indicated fulfills Emerson's description of a friend. Support any generalities you make with specific examples of things that your friend has said or done, times that you've shared, or similar events.

**Thesis**: Write a one-sentence response to the above assignment. Make certain this single sentence offers a clear statement of your position.

*Example: My next-door neighbor and track coach is my "Janus-faced" friend, because she knows the failures and achievements of my past, and because she helps me to overcome uncertainties of the future.*

**Organizational Plan**: If your thesis is the point on which you want to end, where does your essay need to begin? List the points of development that are inevitable in leading your reader from your beginning point to your end point. This list is your outline.

**Draft**: Use your thesis as both your beginning and your end. Following your outline, write a good first draft of your essay. Remember to support all your points with examples, facts, references to reading, etc.

**Review and revise**: Exchange essays with a classmate. Using the scoring guide for Word Choice on page 243, score your partner's essay (while he or she scores yours). Focus on word choice and the use of language conventions. If necessary, rewrite your essay to improve the word choice and/or use of language.

## Improving Paragraphs

*Read the following passage and then answer the multiple-choice questions that follow. The questions will require you to make decisions regarding the revision of the reading selection.*

1    Small town judges are buried in seas of bureaucratic paperwork, and many work from the cramped confines of spare rooms in their own homes.

2    Their judicial accounts, funded by taxpayers and allocated by the town boards, are almost never enough to cover the costs of running these makeshift courts.

3    They work part-time, and they are called upon at any hour of the day. Their courts constitute the first rung of the state's legal ladder, and these elected officials are called upon to handle cases from petit larceny to murder.

4    The judges are not always reluctant to admit they are overworked and underpaid.

5    One judge, for example, says that for his $3200 per year, the state has taken away a lot of his "judgment" and swapped it for a pile of paperwork that needs to be very properly filled out and filed.

6    He said it's more like Russia nowadays. The state sets all the fines and tells you how to judge the cases. Then you spend all your weekends and evenings doing the paperwork. Sometimes more than one evening a week is spent hearing cases. State requirements include two days of schooling every year, for which the only compensation is meals and mileage." A number of judges must take the day off to attend the sessions for which they are tested and "grades" handed down, just like in school.

7    One judge has a day job as supervisor of a state campground. One of the days he must attend justice workshops is during the park's busiest month, so he loses a day's pay. "I guess I'm just fed up," he said, "and when my term is up next year, I will probably not run for re-election. I'm in my third term now, and at about eighty cents an hour, it's not worth it." The gas money that he spends to attend the workshops is more than what the state pays him. He said he originally took the office so he could help people, but with what he terms the state "takeover" of his decisions, he does not feel he can do it anymore.

8    Another justice, on the other hand, would seek re-election for his fourth term because he finds so much satisfaction in the work he does, which he chose to do as a means of serving his fellow human beings. He also conceded that there is a lot of paper work in the job–at least three to four hours "in chambers" for every hour on the bench–and not easily dismissed.

9    He cited the newer judicial system as part of the ever-increasing means to raise money for the state. He said that the surcharges for crimes go as high as $87 for a misdemeanor, $42 for a violation of the penal law, and $25 for traffic or vehicular infractions. Is that a deterrent to committing a crime? The judge didn't think so. He said that the surcharges serve as a means of generating revenue for the state.

1. Which of the following changes would improve the introduction of the article?
   A. Delete paragraph 1.
   B. Combine paragraphs 1, 2, and 3.
   C. Delete paragraph 2.
   D. Exchange paragraphs 2 and 3.
   E. Delete paragraphs 1, 2, and 3.

2. Which of the following changes would best improve continuity within the passage?
   A. Combine paragraphs 1 and 6.
   B. Combine paragraphs 3 and 4.
   C. Combine paragraphs 4 and 5.
   D. Delete paragraph 4.
   E. Exchange paragraphs 4 and 5.

3. Which of the following changes would correct an error in paragraph 6?
   A. Add details about the judge's trip to Russia.
   B. Begin the paragraph with sentence 5.
   C. Omit sentence 1.
   D. Enclose the quoted material with quotation marks.
   E. Delete the reference to Russia in sentence 1.

4. Which of the following sentences could be deleted from paragraph 7 without changing the intent of the paragraph?
   A. sentence 1
   B. sentence 2
   C. sentence 3
   D. sentence 4
   E. sentence 5

5. Which paragraph contradicts the intent of the passage?
   A. paragraph 3
   B. paragraph 4
   C. paragraph 6
   D. paragraph 8
   E. paragraph 9

# REVIEW

## Lessons 1 – 7

### EXERCISE I – Sentence Completion

*Choose the best pair of words to complete the sentence. Most choices will fit grammatically and will even make sense logically, but you must choose the pair that best fits the idea of the sentence.*

*Note that these words are not taken directly from lessons in this book. This exercise is intended to replicate the sentence completion portion of the SAT.*

1. Scientists have long _____ the existence of creatures such as the Loch Ness Monster, and until a previously unknown species appears, the _____ is that these arguments will continue.
   A. examined, extent
   B. questioned, force
   C. calculated, disputing
   D. debated, likelihood
   E. argued, analysis

2. Dora was _____ when she saw a present beneath the Christmas tree, but she spent the day in _____ after learning that the bike was for her older brother.
   A. wondering, jealousy
   B. merriment, complacency
   C. ecstatic, depression
   D. happy, unhappiness
   E. confused, certainty

3. The _____ of his _____ to produce ever-more-complicated liturgical compositions eventually led the eighteenth century composer to cease writing music altogether.
   A. requirements, fans
   B. demands, patrons
   C. needs, creativity
   D. constraints, profession
   E. qualifications, religion

4. _____ to committing the burglary, the thief _____ his disguise, stole a car, and tried to escape, but he was captured when he ran a red light.
   A. Subsequent, destroyed
   B. Wanting, stole
   C. Prior, hid
   D. Trying, purchased
   E. Deciding, constructed

5. "Don't be too rough with your little sister," _____ Mrs. Taylor to her _____ ten-year-old, Katrina.
   A. demanded, daughter
   B. cautioned, rambunctious
   C. screamed, undisciplined
   D. admonished, quivering
   E. said, sadistic

6. Franklin's _____, "A penny saved is a penny earned," meant little to me until I remembered its _____ while discussing allowances with my children.
   A. statement, parsimoniousness
   B. writing, stipulation
   C. quotation, restriction
   D. comment, consequence
   E. aphorism, relevance

7. The Blue Hotel was the last remaining _____ building in the condemned neighborhood, but its owner _____ refused to sell.
   A. old, probably
   B. ramshackle, steadfastly
   C. tired, never
   D. one-room, adamantly
   E. apartment, continuously

8. If it had not been for the _____ errors, the student's _____ paper would have received an *A* instead of a *B+*.
   A. horrible, entire
   B. many, late
   C. mechanical, research
   D. stupid, completed
   E. frequent, mediocre

## EXERCISE II – Crossword Puzzle

*Use the clues to complete the crossword puzzle. The answers consist of vocabulary words from lessons 1 through 7.*

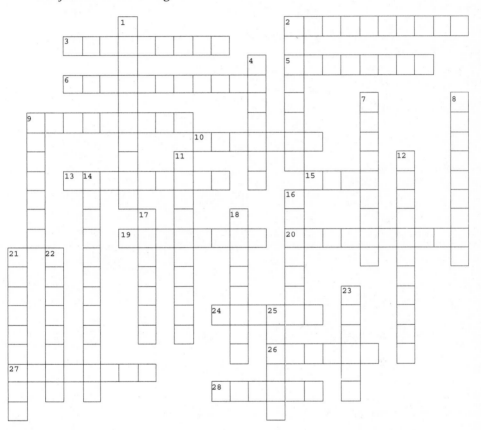

**Across**
2. vulgar
3. respect
5. behavior
6. phony attitude
9. to beg
10. strong disapproval
13. wise
15. rude person
19. hazy
20. exact opposite
24. obvious

26. inexperienced
27. concern for others
28. worn out

**Down**
1. dull
2. hard working
4. burdensome
7. maze
8. violent change
9. shameful
11. happening by chance

12. curse
14. accidental
16. embarrassment
17. complete failure
18. dilemma
21. to clarify
22. to weaken
23. skillful
25. to shun

# Lesson Eight

1.  **deride**  (di rīd´)  *v.*  to ridicule; to mock
    The unpopular professor *derided* students who made mistakes.
    *syn: scorn*                    *ant: praise*

2.  **censure**  (sen´ shər)  *v.*  to criticize sharply
    The judge *censured* the repeat offender for his criminal behavior.
    *syn: condemn; reproach*                    *ant: praise; applaud*

3.  **gambol**  (gam´ bəl)  *v.*  to frolic; to romp about playfully
    The pre-schoolers liked to *gambol* about on the playground.
    *syn: play; caper; rollick*

4.  **immolate**  (im´ ə lāt)  *v.*  to kill someone as a sacrificial victim, usually by fire
    Some Buddhist monks *immolated* themselves in protest of the government's policies.

5.  **recondite**  (rek´ ən dīt)  *adj.*  difficult to understand; profound
    Only a few students understood the *recondite* explanation of the theory.

6.  **martinet**  (mär tn et´)  *n.*  a strict disciplinarian; taskmaster
    The teacher was a *martinet* who never made exceptions to the rules.

7.  **quagmire**  (kwag´ mīr)  *n.*  a swamp; a difficult or inextricable situation
    The war was a political *quagmire* for three U.S. Presidents.

8.  **gibe**  (jīb)  *v.*  to scoff; to ridicule
    His favorite pastime was to *gibe* at everything his wife said.
    *syn: jeer; taunt; sneer*                    *ant: compliment; praise*

9.  **agape**  (ə gāp´)  *adj.*  open-mouthed; surprised; agog
    Even the judge was *agape* when the witness told the ridiculous story in court.
    *syn: astonished*

10. **carcinogen**  (kär sin´ ə jən)  *n.*  causing cancer
    Benzene, a component of gasoline, is a *carcinogen*.

11. **olfactory**  (ol fak´ tə rē)  *adj.*  pertaining to smell
    If you have a cold, then your *olfactory* senses will not detect the gas leak.

12. **imperious** (im pîr´ ē əs) *adj.* domineering; haughty
The judge pronounced his findings in an *imperious* voice.
*syn: overbearing; arrogant; masterful*       *ant: servile; submissive*

13. **grotesque** (grō tesk´ ) *adj.* absurd; distorted
The boy made a *grotesque* face behind the teacher's back.

14. **neologism** (nē äl´ ə jiz əm) *n.* a new word or expression
Some writers coin *neologisms* to confuse and impress their readers.
*syn: coinage*

15. **hackneyed** (hak´ nēd) *adj.* commonplace; overused
"Good as gold" is a *hackneyed* expression.
*syn: trite; banal*                      *ant: fresh; imaginative*


## EXERCISE I—Words in Context

*From the list below, supply the words needed to complete the paragraph. Some words will not be used.*

| | | |
|---|---|---|
| immolate | agape | gibe |
| censure | imperious | martinet |

1.    Janet could not contain herself when the waiter ignored her for the third
time. Like a[n] _____ scolding a naughty schoolboy, Janet stood over
her table and loudly _____ the waiter. _____ patrons at surrounding tables could not believe Janet's _____ outburst, but they
were secretly happy because they, too, were upset with the poor service.
Some of the patrons could not contain their chuckles when Janet angrily
_____ at the manager when he appeared at the table.
    "What do I have to do—_____ myself just to get your attention?
Perhaps you'd see me if I were a human torch!"
    "Please, ma'am; what is the problem here?" asked the manager.

*From the list below, supply the words needed to complete the paragraph. Some words will not be used.*

grotesque        hackneyed        quagmire        gambol
deride             censure           recondite

2.     While most of the second-graders _____ in the playground during recess, Justin spent his time thinking of ways to _____ his teacher. No one—not even Justin—understood his _____ reasons for wanting to complicate Mrs. Nale's life. When asked about Justin's behavior, Mrs. Nale usually responded with the _____ expression, "Boys will be boys." Justin responded by making a[n] _____ face.

*From the list below, supply the words needed to complete the paragraph. Some words will not be used.*

quagmire        censure        carcinogen        immolate
neologism      deride         olfactory         grotesque

3.     The word *bioterrorism* is a[n] _____ that refers to the use of biological agents as terrorist weapons. By themselves, agents such as anthrax and botulism can be invisible to the naked eye and undetectable to the _____ senses. Before cities established emergency management programs, experts believed that the effective release of agents into populated areas would have caused a[n] _____ that overwhelmed every available hospital and emergency worker. Biological and chemical agents would have to be swiftly neutralized; their effects are immediate and severe, unlike those of a mild influenza or the _____ found in water or air pollution.

## EXERCISE II—Sentence Completion

*Complete the sentence in a way that shows you understand the meaning of the italicized vocabulary word.*

1. The editor *censured* Carol's first manuscript, so Carol decided to...

2. The judge did not appreciate it when the defendant *gibed* at...

3. If we had no *olfactory* sense, we would not...

4. *Hackneyed* expressions detract from your writing, so you should...

5. During recess, students *gamboled* on the playground while...

6. Radical supporters sometimes *immolate* themselves in order to...

7. Asbestos is a *carcinogen* that can...

8. Irene made a *grotesque* expression when she took a bite; the food was...

9. Leo's tutor was a *martinet* who made him...

10. We couldn't hear the conversation, but when Will stood there looking *agape*, we knew that he...

11. The coach could not tolerate talented players who *derided*...

12. Jill saw her financial debt as a *quagmire* from which she could...

13. Sandy didn't like to play chess with Patrick, because Patrick made *imperious* remarks every time...

14. People who did not understand the *recondite* reasons for the war decided to...

15. "E-mail" and "spam" are *neologisms* created to describe things that deal with...

## EXERCISE III—Roots, Prefixes, and Suffixes

*Study the entries and answer the questions that follow.*

The suffix *ive* means "relating to" or "tending to."
The roots *ced* and *cess* mean "to yield," "to stop," "to go."
The prefix *pro* means "for."
The prefix *ante* means "before."
The prefix *trans* means "across" or "through."
The root *mot* means "to move."

1.  Using literal translations as guidance, define the following words without using a dictionary.

    A   procession
    B.  antecedent
    C.  process

    D.  transitive
    E.  motive
    F.  massive

2.  A green light signals you to _____ through an intersection.

    Fighting must _____ if warring parties agree on a cessation of combat.

3.  To communicate with someone who speaks a foreign language, you will need to send your message through a[n] _____.

    The transcontinental railroad ran _____ the width of the United States.

4.  List as many words as you can think of that contain the root *mot*.

5.  List as many words as you can think of that contain the roots *ced* or *cess*.

## EXERCISE IV—Inference

*Complete the sentences by inferring information about the italicized word from its context.*

1.  If the theory about hyperspace is *recondite*, then you might need to...

2.  Mom says that schoolteachers used to be strict *martinets*, and now they...

3.  Billy's classmates *derided* him about his clothes the whole time he was in school, so when he finally left the town and found a good job, he...

# EXERCISE V—Critical Reading

*Below is a pair of reading passages followed by several multiple-choice questions similar to the ones you will encounter on the SAT. Carefully read both passages and choose the best answer to each of the questions.*

*The following passages present conflicting opinions about charter schools.*

## Passage 1

1    Many public school boards oppose charter schools, and for obvious reasons: charter schools will set precedents in education that far exceed the capabilities of public schools. Opponents, reluctant to change a failing system, claim that charter schools will have negative effects on communities, but they ignore the positive effects that the schools will have on children—the most important factor.

2    The greatest advantage of charter schools is that the administrators do not have their hands tied by the state in matters of funds and curriculum. Instead of wasting tax dollars on programs that might or might not need to be fixed, charter school administrators can decide where the funds truly need to be directed. If administrators believe that students need more technology, they can simply allocate the funds to meet the needs of the students instead of slogging through the levels of bureaucracy required for even common sense decisions. Administrators also have the authority to choose curricula that exceed the minimum requirements set by state guidelines; for example, if seventh graders are working at a ninth grade level, then administrators can authorize the teaching of advanced material. Instead of hammering achievers down to average levels, charter schools pull underachievers up to challenging levels.

3    Charter schools provide valuable alternatives to public schools and teachers. Many charter schools specialize in specific programs of education, such as art, science, or technology. By directing the appropriate students to specialized schools, public schools can unload the burden of dividing limited funds into small but necessary programs. Teachers at charter schools have the opportunity to employ more creative lesson plans and effective teaching methods, all to the advantage of the students.

4    Charter schools also provide an incentive for public schools to make long-needed improvements. If public schools experience an emigration of students, then they will be forced to address the problems that drive students to charter schools. Public school environments, teaching methods, and curricula will need to be reevaluated and improved; otherwise, the schools will be condemned as wastes of tax dollars. The rivalry will force public schools to meet education standards or simply get out of the way. If they rise to the occasion and match the quality of education available at charter schools, then students in both types of schools will benefit.

5    Charter schools eliminate the red tape that entangles public funds and education guidelines, and this ability clearly gives them an advantage over public schools. Students will be challenged, teachers will have their shackles removed, and public schools will have to improve in order to stay in the race to properly educate children. The creation of charter schools is clearly a win-win situation.

## Passage 2

1    Charter schools are detrimental to an education system that has improved since its conception. They will probably inhibit public schools and devalue education as a whole. Communities should help children by investing in public schools instead of abandoning a perfectly good system.

2    The charter school is such a new concept that no one knows what types of problems it might cause. Inexperienced administrators could issue erroneous reports or fail to discover problems that impede learning. Fraudulent administrators, operating charter schools under relaxed state scrutiny, might fail to report harmful problems to the proper authorities. The complexity of educational bureaucracy in public schools is intentional and necessary; through redundancy, it creates safeguards that ensure a safe learning environment for children. Granting autonomy to administrators at charter schools endangers the children.

3    Charter schools also create animosity in communities. Rivalries may result between charter school students and public school students. Public school students may ostracize charter school students because they perceive charter school students as acting superior. Parents might behave in the same way; parents of public school students might develop contempt for charter schools because they route money from public schools and thus away from public school students.

4    As charter schools proliferate, public schools might become dumping grounds for aberrant students. When students get expelled from charter schools, they will be sent to regular public schools, thereby giving the impression that public schools harbor "rejects" who do not attend school to learn. Existing students in public schools will then view themselves as rejects, since they are attending the dumping ground instead of the "elite" charter school. Confidence will be diminished, and the compromise in self-image will be detrimental to good students.

5    Charter schools will put teachers, students, and even parents at odds with their peers. The children, of course, will be the victims, because they will be forfeiting their early education and thus the foundation for future education and achievement. They will gain only low self-esteem and inferior educations, and it will prove that charter schools should never have been implemented.

1. The overall tone of the first passage is
   A. condemning.
   B. affirmative.
   C. sympathetic.
   D. negative.
   E. ironic.

2. According to the first passage, which of the following is the most important advantage of charter schools?
   A. valuable alternative to public school
   B. autonomous administration
   C. more funds available
   D. incentive for public schools to improve
   E. no leg irons

3. Which of the suggestions best paraphrases the following quotation in the context of the passage?

   > Instead of hammering achievers down to average levels, charter schools pull underachievers up to challenging levels.

   A. Public schools stifle their best students.
   B. Public schools have average programs.
   C. Charter schools challenge both average and above-average students.
   D. Charter schools and public schools vary.
   E. Charter schools provide hammers to build level challenges.

4. According to the first passage, public schools will be condemned if
   A. too many people decide to attend charter schools.
   B. they take over closing charter school facilities.
   C. the state does not provide funds to increase teacher salaries.
   D. they fail to match the standards of charter schools.
   E. buildings become unstable due to high cost of maintenance.

5. As used in paragraph 4 of the first passage, *emigration* most nearly means
   A. departure.
   B. return.
   C. failure rate.
   D. foreign exchange.
   E. flood.

6. As used in paragraph 4 of the second passage, *aberrant* most nearly means
   A. terrible.
   B. handicapped.
   C. advanced.
   D. proper.
   E. deviant.

7. According to the second passage, which of the following is *not* a reason that charter schools are detrimental to education?
   A. community bitterness
   B. diminished student confidence
   C. inexperienced administrators
   D. higher school taxes
   E. failure to address problems

8. As used in paragraph 4 of the second passage, *proliferate* most nearly means
   A. multiply.
   B. decrease.
   C. envelop.
   D. advertise.
   E. overrun.

9. Which of the following subtopics is used as support in both passages, but for opposite reasons?
   A. having specific curriculum options
   B. properly distributing state funds
   C. animosity in communities
   D. disposition of aberrant students
   E. granting autonomy to schools

10. Which of the following best compares the tone of both passages?
    A. The authors of both passages suggest that they favor charter schools.
    B. Passage 1 has a confident tone, while passage 2 is uncertain.
    C. The passages are identical in tone.
    D. The tone of passage 1 has the opposite effect of the tone of passage 2.
    E. Passage 1 entreats readers, while passage 2 instructs readers.

# Lesson Nine

1.  **machination** (mak ə nā´ shən)  *n.*  an evil design or plan
    Once again, the superhero foiled the *machinations* of the evil scientist.
    *syn: scheme; plot*

2.  **pejorative** (pi jôr´ə tiv)  *adj.*  having a negative effect; insulting
    Lenny resigned after overhearing his coworkers' *pejorative* remarks.
    *syn: disparaging; derogatory*          *ant: complimentary*

3.  **harbinger** (här´ bin jər)  *n.*  an omen or sign
    To many, the black cat is a *harbinger* of bad luck.
    *syn: warning; portent*

4.  **nubile** (nōō´ bīl)  *adj.*  suitable for marriage in age and physical
       development, referring to a female
    In six years, she grew from a skinny twelve-year-old to a *nubile* young
    woman.

5.  **sapient** (sā´pi ənt)  *adj.*  wise; full of knowledge
    Everyone sought advice from the *sapient* monk who lived on the mountain.
    *syn: sagacious*          *ant: fatuous; inane*

6.  **chimerical** (kə mer´ i kəl)  *adj.*  imaginary; fantastic
    Little Tina had a *chimerical* notion that rabbits lived in trees.
    *syn: absurd; illusionary*          *ant: practical*

7.  **masochist** (mas´ə kist)  *n.*  one who enjoys his or her own pain and
       suffering
    Sue accused her friend of being a *masochist* because he refused to go to the
    doctor despite his broken toes.

8.  **finesse** (fi nes´)  *n.*  diplomacy; tact; artful management
    The diplomat had the *finesse* to deal with the troublesome nation.
    *syn: skill; cunning*          *ant: tactlessness*

9.  **heterogeneous** (het ər ə jē´ nē əs)  *adj.*  different; dissimilar
    The platoon was a *heterogeneous* group of young men from various back-
    grounds.
    *syn: diverse; varied*          *ant: homogeneous; similar*

10. **eclectic** (e klek´ tik)  *adj.*  choosing from various sources
    The *eclectic* furnishings were from many different nations and historical
    periods.
    *syn: selective*          *ant: narrow*

11. **grandiose**  (gran´ dē ōs)  *adj.*  impressive; showy; magnificent
The young couple could not afford the *grandiose* home, so they found a smaller house.
*syn: stately; imposing*                          *ant: humble*

12. **raiment**  (rā´ mənt)  *n.*  clothing; garments
The royal *raiment* of the princess is copied by the fashion industry for the department-store market.

13. **blanch**  (blanch)  *v.*  to whiten; to make pale
Sue's face *blanched* when she saw the charred remains of her house.

14. **hybrid**  (hī´ brid)  *n.*  anything of mixed origin
The *hybrid* roses had the best traits of two different species.

15. **idiosyncrasy**  (id ē ō sing´ krə sē)  *n.*  a peculiar personality trait
Hiding money in tin cans was only one of the old man's *idiosyncrasies*.
*syn: eccentricity; quirk*

## EXERCISE I—Words in Context

*From the list below, supply the words needed to complete the paragraph. Some words will not be used.*

| | | | |
|---|---|---|---|
| sapient | idiosyncrasy | blanch | machination |
| pejorative | masochist | nubile | heterogeneous |
| grandiose | raiment | finesse | |

1.  Dr. Quade still wore the _____ of a maximum-security prison inmate when he entered an abandoned warehouse to evade the searchlights of police helicopters. Six years of living without sunlight in an underground cell had _____ the color of his face, and the _____ treatment that he received from guards had left him with a perpetual scowl. Now, he mused, he would be free to carry out the _____ that he had planned during his confinement, but not before using his criminal _____ to steal an automobile from the nearby parking garage. The garage contained a[n] _____ collection of automobiles, but the _____ Dr. Quade chose a very dull, plain car to hotwire; a[n] _____ car could draw unwanted attention that jeopardized the escape.

    Even without keys, the mad genius was able to start the car in two minutes; however, he revealed a violent _____ by punching the dashboard when a light indicated that the car was low in fuel. The resulting cuts on his hands would have irritated a normal person, but not a[n] _____ like Dr. Quade.

*From the list below, supply the words needed to complete the paragraph. Some words will not be used.*

| | | | |
|---|---|---|---|
| hybrid | idiosyncrasy | harbinger | raiment |
| eclectic | nubile | chimerical | |

2.  Robin's _____ art collection included paintings and sculptures from all over the world. Her favorite painting, *Consumption*, depicts a[n] _____ young woman in Victorian clothing standing amid a courtyard flower garden. A close look at the garden reveals poppies, a cypress tree, and tiny white butterflies, all of which are symbolic as _____ of illness or death. The artist painted the _____ scene during a tuberculosis epidemic, apparently to depict the ruthlessness of the illness. Robin calls *Consumption* a[n] _____, because the painting is simultaneously pleasing and depressing.

## EXERCISE II—Sentence Completion

*Complete the sentence in a way that shows you understand the meaning of the italicized vocabulary word.*

1. Henson's daughter had grown into a *nubile* young woman, so the lonely Trader Bill asked...

2. The receptionist at the complaint department lacked the *finesse* to...

3. Aaron was afraid of heights, so his face *blanched* when...

4. Good friends seldom allow an *idiosyncrasy* to...

5. Shouting *pejorative* remarks to the other team will not...

6. Madeline, who just turned two, has the *chimerical* notion that...

7. Plant *hybrids*, like tangelos, are grown by combining...

8. Compared to the elegant *raiment* of the Victorian era, the mass-produced clothing of modern society is...

9. One *harbinger* of an approaching storm is...

10. Mom has only knickknacks, but Tiffany's *eclectic* collection includes...

11. Don't consider yourself to be *sapient* just because you...

12. Ned and Mary wanted to buy the *grandiose* mansion on the hill, but they...

13. Luckily, Captain Freedom foiled Dr. X's evil *machinations* to...

14. In weather this frigid, only a *masochist* would want to...

15. Within the jiggling block of lime gelatin was a *heterogeneous* mixture of...

## EXERCISE III—Roots, Prefixes, and Suffixes

*Study the entries and answer the questions that follow.*

The prefix *dia* means "across."
The roots *vad* and *vas* mean "go."
The roots *trud* and *trus* mean "thrust."
The root *verb* means "word."
The root *ab* means "away" or "from."
The suffix *gram* means "written."
The suffix *meter* means "measure."
The root *tele* means "afar."

1.  Using literal translations as guidance, define the following words without using a dictionary.

    A.  diameter       D.  invade
    B.  diagram        E.  evasive
    C.  speedometer    F.  telegram

2.  Literally, if you *intrude*, you _____, so the word *obtrusion* probably means _____.

    The word *abstruse* contains the root *trus*, but the word means "difficult to understand." Explain how *abstruse* might have acquired its meaning.

3.  If you repeat someone word for word, then you quote that person _____.

    If you are _____, then you use too many words; if you commit *verbicide*, then you _____.

4.  List as many words as you can think of that contain the root *ab*.

5.  List as many words as you can think of that contain the root *gram*.

## EXERCISE IV—Inference

*Complete the sentences by inferring information about the italicized word from its context.*

1.  The soldier's combat *raiment* contrasted with the native attire because it...

2.  The ambassador's lack of *finesse* in dealing with the hostile forces caused...

3.  Nancy did not like her employer, but she never made *pejorative* comments because she knew that it would...

## EXERCISE V—Writing

*Here is a writing prompt similar to the one you will find on the writing portion of the SAT.*

Plan and write an essay based on the following statement:

> In Henrik Ibsen's *A Doll's House*, Nora, a middle-class wife who struggles to find her identity, is confronted with what "defines" her. Responding to her husband, who has just told her that she is first a wife and then a mother, Nora states, "I don't believe in that anymore. I believe that, before all else, I'm a human being, no less than you—or anyway, I ought to try to become one. I know that the majority thinks you're right, Torvald, and plenty of books agree with you, too. But I can't go on believing what the majority says, or what's written in books."
> –An excerpt from *A Doll's House*, 1879

**Assignment**: Write an essay in which you discuss the ways in which society tries to define people. Consider how the roles imposed by society restrict or aid the lives of individuals. Support your position with examples from literature, history, personal observations, or experiences.

**Thesis**: Write a one-sentence response to the above assignment. Make certain this single sentence offers a clear statement of your position.

*Example: Just as Nora finds herself pigeonholed in the role of wife and mother in Henrik Isben's* A Doll's House, *we are all categorized in some way and then stereotyped based on that category.*

**Organizational Plan**: If your thesis is the point on which you want to end, where does your essay need to begin? List the points of development that are inevitable in leading your reader from your beginning point to your end point. This list is your outline.

**Draft**: Use your thesis as both your beginning and your end. Following your outline, write a good first draft of your essay. Remember to support all your points with examples, facts, references to reading, etc.

**Review and revise**: Exchange essays with a classmate. Using the Holistic scoring guide on page 244, score your partner's essay (while he or she scores yours). If necessary, rewrite your essay to correct the problems indicated by the essay's score.

## Identifying Sentence Errors

*Identify the grammatical error in each of the following sentences. If the sentence contains no error, select answer choice E.*

1.  After spending the day at the amusement park, the children, who
                 (A)                                        (B)
    normally beg to stay up past their bedtime, was eager to climb into their
                              (C)                 (D)
    beds.     No error
              (E)

2.  After a long day at the office, the chairman arrived at home to find a
                             (A)                  (B)
    dozen papers that needed his signature of approval  lying on his desk.
                        (C)                         (D)
    No error
      (E)

3.  During French class, the students were taught that the word *aimer*
             (A)               (B)                 (C)
    is when you like a person.   No error
      (D)                 (E)

4.  Alot of people   who come to the United States from Asian countries
      (A)                          (B)
    have a hard time adjusting to Americans who wear shoes when
    (C)                                  (D)
    entering homes.   No error
                (E)

5.  Susie, who is notorious for finding the best bargains at the mall, bought
                     (A)
    the following, a sweater to wear to the bonfire, three pairs of mittens for
          (B)               (C)
    the parade, and suede jeans and a silk blouse for the dance.  No error
              (D)                     (E)

# Improving Sentences

*The underlined portion of each sentence below contains some flaw. Select the answer choice that best corrects the flaw.*

6.  To gain a better view of the stars in the Grand Canyon, the astronomer adjusts his lens and then continued to monitor the meteor shower for his research.
    A.  To gain a better view of the stars in the Grand Canyon the astronomer adjusts his lens and then continued to monitor the meteor shower for his research.
    B.  To gain a better view of the stars in the Grand Canyon, the astronomer adjusted his lens and then continued to monitor the meteor shower for his research.
    C.  To gain a better view of the stars from the Grand Canyon, the astronomer adjusted his lens, and then continued to monitor the meteor shower for his research.
    D.  In order to gain a better view of the stars in the Grand Canyon, the astronomer adjusted his lens and then continued to monitor the meteor shower for his research.
    E.  Gaining a better view of the stars in the Grand Canyon, the astronomer adjusts his lens and then continued to monitor the meteor shower for his research.

7.  Finding the perfect pet requires researching, planning, and to purchase the necessary supplies.
    A.  research, planning, and the purchase of necessary supplies.
    B.  researching, planning, and purchasing the necessary supplies.
    C.  planning and researching supplies that will be necessary.
    D.  supplies, in addition to research and planning.
    E.  researching and planning which supplies to purchase.

8.  To find his bone, underneath the bush the dog sniffed while his master waited nearby.
    A.  To find his bone while his master waited nearby, underneath the bush the dog sniffed.
    B.  To find his bone while his master waited nearby, underneath the bush the dog sniffed to find his bone.
    C.  The dog sniffed to find his bone underneath the bush while his master waited nearby.
    D.  The dog sniffed while his master waited nearby to find his bone underneath the bush.
    E.  While his master waited nearby, the dog sniffed underneath the bush to find his bone.

9. A large suggestion box has been placed in the corridor outside the supervisor's office, <u>shoppers can render their suggestions and concerns about the mall.</u>
   A. where shoppers can render their suggestions and concerns about the mall.
   B. where shoppers can render their suggestions and concerns about the mall, in this way.
   C. in this way, shoppers can render their suggestions and concerns about the mall.
   D. shoppers can use this to render their suggestions and concerns about the mall.
   E. to render their suggestions and concerns about the mall, shoppers can use this.

10. <u>The concert was finished at midnight, and no one went home.</u>
   A. The concert was finished at midnight, moreover no one went home.
   B. The concert was finished at midnight, yet no one went home.
   C. The concert was finished at midnight, consequently no one went home.
   D. The concert was finished at midnight, no one went home.
   E. The concert was finished at midnight, hence no one went home.

# Lesson Ten

1. **idolatry** (ī dol´ ə trē) *n.* excessive or blind adoration; worship of an object
   The priest accused them of *idolatry* for worshipping a statue.

2. **adulterate** (ə dul´ tə rāt) *v.* to make impure; to contaminate
   The fumes from the automobiles *adulterate* the air.
   *syn: taint; corrupt*          *ant: refine; refined*

3. **emanate** (em´ ə nāt) *v.* to come forth; to send forth
   She tried to control her anger, but harsh words began to *emanate* from her lips.
   *syn: rise; emerge*

4. **garish** (gar´ ish) *adj.* tastelessly gaudy
   The gypsy costumes were too *garish* for my taste.
   *syn: showy; glaring; flashy*          *ant: sedate; conservative*

5. **immutable** (i myōō´ tə bəl) *adj.* unchangeable; fixed
   The laws of nature are *immutable*.
   *syn: enduring*          *ant: flexible; changeable*

6. **diadem** (dī´ ə dem´) *n.* a crown
   Peter referred to his wife's blonde hair as her golden *diadem*.

7. **bucolic** (byōō kol´ ik) *adj.* pertaining to the countryside; rural; rustic
   The *bucolic* setting of the old inn made it a popular retreat from the city.
   *syn: pastoral*          *ant: urban*

8. **redolent** (red´ ə lənt) *adj.* having a pleasant odor; suggestive or evocative
   The new fabric softener is advertised as being *redolent* of a spring day.
   *syn: aromatic*          *ant: acrid*

9. **impecunious** (im pi kyōō´ nē əs) *adj.* without money; penniless
   Though *impecunious*, the man's pride prevented him from asking for help.
   *syn: destitute; indigent*          *ant: affluent; prosperous*

10. **sedition** (si dish´ ən) *n.* rebellion or resistance against the government
    The rebels were charged with *sedition* when they protested the new dictator.
    *syn: treachery; disloyalty*

11. **defile**   (di fīl´)   *v.*   to pollute; to corrupt
    The oil spill *defiled* the entire bay.

12. **gratuitous**   (grə tōō´ i təs)   *adj.*   unnecessary or uncalled for
    He always gave *gratuitous* advice whether someone wanted it or not.

13. **onus**   (ō´ nəs)   *n.*   a burden; a responsibility
    When father died, Jake had the *onus* of running the farm.
    *syn: obligation*

14. **impious**   (im´ pē əs)   *adj.*   disrespectful toward God
    Some consider laughing in church to be *impious* behavior.
    *syn: irreligious; profane*                    *ant: devout; pious*

15. **caveat**   (kā´ vi at)   *n.*   a warning
    John had so much confidence in his ability that he did not heed the old
    *caveat* about swimming alone.
    *syn: admonition; caution*

## EXERCISE I—Words in Context

*From the list below, supply the words needed to complete the paragraph. Some words will not be used.*

| | | | |
|---|---|---|---|
| immutable | bucolic | gratuitous | adulterate |
| sedition | impecunious | defile | redolent |
| emanate | garish | | |

1.  Mike dreamed of leaving the city and returning to the _____ area where he was raised; however, his wife's opinion remained _____, and she refused to move beyond the suburbs.

    "How can you stand to live here and let the crime and pollution _____ our family?" Mike argued.

    Tara's usual opposition _____ from her mouth with little effort. "I'd rather let the smog and the crooks _____ the quality of life than the termites and mosquitoes that live in that _____ shack in the country."

    "But just imagine," Mike pleaded, "stepping outside in the morning and inhaling the air _____ of a fresh bouquet." He added _____ deep-breathing noises and satisfied "Ahhs" to make his point.

    Tara looked at him. "We would both have to sacrifice good jobs, and there's little employment out there. I really don't want a[n] _____ life after we've worked so hard to have nice things."

*From the list below, supply the words needed to complete the paragraph. Some words will not be used.*

| | | | |
|---|---|---|---|
| onus | redolent | diadem | idolatry |
| caveat | impious | sedition | bucolic |

2.  The gold rush town existed solely for the _____ of the rare, yellow metal. Reverend Jerry, who arrived yesterday with the _____ of building a congregation, immediately issued _____ to the _____ establishments on Main Street, specifically the saloon and the brothel. He hoped that over time he could inspire a[n] _____ against the crooked politicians and greedy entrepreneurs that ran the boomtown; if he succeeded, Dobson City would be the _____ of the reverend's many achievements.

## EXERCISE II—Sentence Completion

*Complete the sentence in a way that shows you understand the meaning of the italicized vocabulary word.*

1.  Tim's mom let us borrow her car, but she included the *caveat* that if…

2.  *Gratuitous* handshaking is a normal routine for…

3.  The *impecunious* family experienced a change in lifestyle when…

4.  Sometimes, a fascination with television is a form of *idolatry*, because we…

5.  After the battle, the commander had the *onus* of…

6.  Some people wanted to charge the protestors with *sedition* when they…

7.  The guards took the king's *diadem* before they took him to…

8.  Leroy, who thought he was being helpful, *adulterated* the recipe by…

9.  Gina did not like spending summer in the *bucolic* setting because…

10. In colonial Salem, Massachusetts, people who committed *impious* acts were…

11. The crime boss had *immutable* authority over the town until…

12. When the neighbor's loud music *emanated* through the ceiling of the apartment, Mandy reacted by…

13. Crude oil *defiled* the bay when the captain of the tanker…

14. Lisa had a broken leg, but the *redolent* flowers next to her bed helped…

15. Everyone stared at Barbara's *garish* outfit when she…

# EXERCISE III—Roots, Prefixes, and Suffixes

*Study the entries and answer the questions that follow.*

The roots *leg, lig,* and *lect* mean "to choose," "to read," or "to gather."
The root *neg* means "to deny."
The prefix *e* means "out" or "from."
The prefix *re* means "again."
The prefix *se* means "apart."
The suffix *ion* means "the act of."

1.  Using literal translations as guidance, define the following words without using a dictionary.

    A. legible           D. negate
    B. legion            E. neglect
    C. renegade          F. elect

2.  A[n] _____ is a person who chooses specific items or types of items to gather. They often _____ items to gather by choosing the things that they need to complete whole sets.

3.  The professor should know better than to _____ students for three hours without taking a break. He put forth so much information that few can _____, or *remember*, the subjects covered during the beginning of the speech.

4.  If you deny a promise that you made to purchase something, you are said to _____ on the deal.

5.  The word *legend* contains a root that means "to read." Explain the possible reason for the word *legend* containing the root *leg*.

## EXERCISE IV—Inference

*Complete the sentences by inferring information about the italicized word from its context.*

1.  As cities expand, *bucolic* areas that once featured barns and old forests are now host to…

2.  You should have taken seriously my *caveat* about speeding, because now you are…

3.  Ernest was Blake's best friend, so when Blake died in combat, Ernest had the *onus* of…

## EXERCISE V—Critical Reading

*Below is a reading passage followed by several multiple-choice questions similar to the ones you will encounter on the SAT. Carefully read the passage and choose the best answer to each of the questions.*

*Alice Meynell (1847-1922), was an English poet and writer. The following passage reveals her perspective on what she describes as "decivilized" nations.*

The difficulty of dealing—in the course of any critical duty—with decivilized man lies in this: when you accuse him of vulgarity—sparing him no doubt the word—he defends himself against the charge of barbarism. Especially from new soil—remote, colonial—he faces you, bronzed, with a half conviction of savagery,
5   partly persuaded of his own youthfulness of race. He writes, and recites, poems about ranches and canyons; they are designed to betray the recklessness of his nature and to reveal the good that lurks in the lawless ways of a young society. He is there to explain himself, voluble, with a glossary for his own artless slang. But his colonialism is only provincialism very articulate. The new air does but make old
10  decadences seem more stale; the young soil does but set into fresh conditions the ready-made, the uncostly, the refuse feeling of a race decivilizing. He who played long this pattering part of youth, hastened to assure you with so self-denying a face he did not wear war-paint and feathers, that it became doubly difficult to communicate to him that you had suspected him of nothing wilder than a second-hand
15  (figurative) dress coat. And when it was a question not of rebuke, but of praise, even the American was ill-content with the word of the judicious who lauded him for some delicate successes in continuing something of the literature of England, something of the art of France; he was more eager for the applause that stimulated him to write poems in prose form and to paint panoramic landscape, after brief
20  training in academies of native inspiration. Even now English voices are constantly calling upon America to begin—to begin, for the world is expectant. Whereas

there is no beginning for her, but instead a fine and admirable continuity which only a constant care can guide into sustained advance.

But decivilized man is not peculiar to new soil. The English town, too, knows
25 him in all his dailiness. In England, too, he has a literature, an art, a music, all his own—derived from many and various things of price. Trash, in the fullness of its insimplicity and cheapness, is impossible without a beautiful past. Its chief characteristic—which is futility, not failure—could not be achieved but by the long abuse, the rotatory reproduction, the quotidian disgrace, of the utterances of Art,
30 especially the utterance by words. Gaiety, vigour, vitality, the organic quality, purity, simplicity, precision—all these are among the antecedents of trash. It is after them; it is also, alas, because of them. And nothing can be much sadder that such a proof of what may possibly be the failure of derivation.

Evidently we cannot choose our posterity. Reversing the steps of time, we may,
35 indeed choose backwards. We may give our thoughts noble forefathers. Well begotten, well born our fancies must be; they shall be also well derived. We have a voice in decreeing our inheritance, and not our inheritance only, but our heredity. Our minds may trace upwards and follow their ways to the best well-heads of the arts. The very habit of our thoughts may be persuaded one way unawares by their ante-
40 natal history. Their companions must be lovely, but need be no lovelier than their ancestors; and being so fathered and so husbanded, our thoughts may be intrusted to keep the counsels of literature.

Such is our confidence in a descent we know. But, of a sequel which of us is sure? Which of us is secured against the dangers of subsequent depreciation? And, more-
45 over, which of us shall trace the contemporary tendencies, the one towards honour, the other towards dishonour? Or who shall discover why derivation becomes degeneration, and where and when and how the bastardy befalls? The decivilized have every grace as the antecedent of their vulgarities, every distinction as the precedent of their mediocrities. No ballad-concert song, feign it sigh, frolic, or
50 laugh, but has the excuse that the feint was suggested, was made easy, by some living sweetness once. Nor are the decivilized to blame as having in their own persons possessed civilization and marred it. They did not possess it; they were born into some tendency to derogation, into an inclination for things mentally inexpensive. And the tendency can hardly do other than continue.

55 Nothing can look duller than the future of this second-hand and multiplying world. Men need not be common merely because they are many; but the infection of commonness once begun in the many, what dullness in their future! To the eye that has reluctantly discovered this truth—that the vulgarized are not un-civilized, and that there is no growth for them—it does not look like a future at all. More bal-
60 lad-concerts, more quaint English, more robustious barytone songs, more piecemeal pictures, more colonial poetry, more young nations with withered traditions. Yet it is before this prospect that the provincial overseas lifts up his voice in a boast or a promise common enough among the incapable young, but pardonable only in senility. He promises the world a literature, an art, that shall be new because his for-
65 est is untracked and his town just built. But what the newness is to be he cannot tell. Certain words were dreadful once in the mouth of desperate old age. Dreadful and pitiable as the threat of an impotent king, what shall we name them when they are the promise of an impotent people? "I will do such things: what they are yet I know not."

1. Through the author's use of the phrase *artless slang* in line 8, a reader can infer that
   A. the author has never left England.
   B. colonists speak in monotones.
   C. the author does not admire the colonial dialect.
   D. the passage is written for artists.
   E. the author is a professor of language.

2. Line 9 suggests that colonial status is
   A. equal to provincial status.
   B. favorable to provincial status.
   C. worse than provincial status.
   D. not as articulate as provincial status.
   E. sought by most provincial inhabitants.

3. Which best paraphrases the following quotation?

   > Whereas there is no beginning for her [America], but instead a fine and admirable continuity which only a constant care can guide into sustained advance.

   A. Europeans are experts in colonization.
   B. American culture has no real beginning; it is simply a continuation of English culture, and it requires guidance in order to properly advance.
   C. No one has traced ancient American history far enough to determine when the continent was first settled.
   D. English culture is the foundation for any nation that began as a colony, except for America.
   E. America will fail without the help of England.

4. Where, according to the author, can "decivilized men" be found?
   A. England and France
   B. America and France
   C. Germany and Canada
   D. West Virginia and England
   E. American and English towns

5. In line 33, *failure of derivation* refers to
   A. the failure to prevent the spread of English art.
   B. the failure to improve upon existing cultural achievements.
   C. the failure to acknowledge the history of trash.
   D. the failure to apply higher mathematics to the arts.
   E. the failure to stop the reproduction of European art and literature.

6. In the third paragraph, the author suggests traveling backwards in time for the purpose of
   A. protecting art and literature traditions from corruption.
   B. warning ancestors about the destiny of their achievements.
   C. learning the art secrets of ancestors.
   D. persuading colonists to abstain from dabbling in art and literature.
   E. escaping a dire present time.

7. According to the fourth paragraph, why should the decivilized not be blamed for defiling civilization?
   A. Decivilized people do not know right from wrong.
   B. They never actually had civilization, so they couldn't have ruined it.
   C. They began their civilization from scratch.
   D. Decivilized people are instructed by errant founding fathers.
   E. They lacked any formal education programs.

8. As used in line 53, *derogation* most nearly means
   A. indifference toward other people.
   B. willingness to try new things.
   C. adaptation to austere climates.
   D. degradation of standards.
   E. defense of their own ways.

9. Which of the following best describes the tone of this passage?
   A. affectionate
   B. condescending
   C. detached
   D. affectionate
   E. scathing

10. The purpose of this passage is to
    A. belittle the traditions of colonists.
    B. explain the differences between colonies and provinces.
    C. inform about the cessation of progress in civilization.
    D. entertain through satire.
    E. argue against granting statehood to the colonies.

# Lesson Eleven

1. **elixir** (i lik´ sər)  *n.*  a supposed remedy for all ailments
The old woman had a secret *elixir* that she claimed would cure a cold in a day.
*syn: medicine; panacea*

2. **desiccated**  (des´ i kāt´ d)  *adj.*  dried up
When she opened the old scrapbook, a *desiccated* rose fell to the floor.

3. **cessation**  (se sā´ shən)  *n.*  a stopping; a discontinuance
There was a *cessation* in the battle, but everyone knew that the shooting would begin again.
*syn: ceasing; end*                    *ant: beginning; commencement*

4. **juxtapose**  (juk stə pōz´)  *v.*  to place side-by-side for comparison
To weigh your options, *juxtapose* the good things with the bad.
*syn: measure; examine*

5. **kinetic**  (ki net´ ik)  *adj.*  pertaining to motion
To demonstrate *kinetic* energy, he threw a steel ball across the lab.

6. **garrulous**  (gar´ ə ləs)  *adj.*  talkative
We didn't think that the *garrulous* salesman would ever leave.
*syn: loquacious; verbose*                    *ant: taciturn*

7. **fetish**  (fet´ ish)  *n.*  an object that receives respect or devotion
The totem pole was a *fetish* of the tribe.
*syn: charm; talisman*

8. **scintillate**  (sin´ til āt)  *v.*  to sparkle; to twinkle; to sparkle intellectually
The lights *scintillated* throughout the otherwise drab room.

9. **lachrymose**  (lak´ rə mōs)  *adj.*  tearful, weepy
It was time for Debbie to get over her *lachrymose* behavior and start smiling again.

10. **fissure**  (fish´ ər)  *n.*  an opening; a groove; a split
The earthquake created *fissures* that swallowed cars and buildings.

11. **epitome**  (i pit´ ə mē)  *n.*  a typical example
As she attended to the comfort of her guests, she was the *epitome* of Southern hospitality.
*syn: embodiment; archetype*

12. **languid** (lang´ gwid)  *adj.*  sluggish; drooping from weakness
    The hot summer day made everyone *languid.*
    *syn: listless; feeble; drooping*                *ant: robust; vigorous*

13. **delineate**  (di lin´ ē āt)  *v.*  to describe, to depict
    The politician *delineated* his disarmament proposal in great detail.

14. **legerdemain**  (lej´ ər di mān´)  *n.*  sleight of hand; deception
    The magician's act was an extraordinary feat of *legerdemain.*

15. **libertine**  (lib´ ər tēn)  *n.*  one who leads an immoral life
    He pretended to be righteous during the day, but he was a *libertine* at night.
    *syn: hedonist; glutton; epicurean*

## EXERCISE I—Words in Context

*From the list below, supply the words needed to complete the paragraph. Some words will not be used.*

| | | | |
|---|---|---|---|
| delineate | fissure | juxtapose | cessation |
| fetish | kinetic | epitome | elixir |
| desiccated | garrulous | libertine | |

1.    The _____ members of the city planning council chatted about the proposed casino to be built just beyond the city limits. The _____ of the arguments against construction _____ the casino as a[n] _____ that would attract _____ who thrive on the crime associated with gambling.

"Well of course the idea sounds bad if you _____ gambling and its patrons like that," said Mr. Taylor. "But in reality, it will be normal, everyday people who benefit from the tax revenues of the casino—not kingpins and mobsters. We are already facing a loss of revenue from the _____ of production at the local glass factory. Our _____ maintenance budget needs to be replenished, and the casino would do just that."

Ms. Hartford spoke in response. "I know that the city is suffering, but the casino is not a[n] _____ that could instantly cure our unemployment problem. It would only make up for half of the jobs lost at the factory."

The proposed casino had caused a[n] _____ in the council; it would take the council three additional meetings to make a final decision.

*From the list below, supply the words needed to complete the paragraph. Some words will not be used.*

| | | | |
|---|---|---|---|
| legerdemain | kinetic | juxtapose | scintillate |
| lachrymose | languid | fissure | |

2.    Madeline cried when she scratched her knee, but her _____ expression disappeared when her grandpa sat down in the swing beside her. Her eyes, still damp, _____ beneath the bright June sun, and she stared in amazement when grandpa used _____ to make it appear as though he pulled a quarter from behind Madeline's ear. Madeline smiled, jumped out of the swing, and ran to the sandbox. Grandpa, _____ from the oppressive heat, marveled at his granddaughter's constant _____ play; Madeline appeared to have limitless energy, even on such a hot day.

## EXERCISE II—Sentence Completion

*Complete the sentence in a way that shows you understand the meaning of the italicized vocabulary word.*

1.  I knew the *elixir* was a scam because…

2.  The *cessation* of the riot occurred when…

3.  A falling brick has more *kinetic* energy than…

4.  Clive liked most classic automobiles, but his *fetish* was…

5.  Tammy was *lachrymose* for two days after her cat…

6.  People called Theresa the *epitome* of human compassion because she…

7.  Dr. Ripper, the special weapons program director, *delineated* his plan to…

8.  Mayor Giuliani closed the shops that attracted *libertines* to Center City because he…

9.  The *desiccated* grease on the bearings of the motor caused it to…

10. The senator *juxtaposed* the landfill and recent complaints from the community in order to…

11. Mr. Foster snapped when the *garrulous* students refused to…

12. The sequins on the prom dress *scintillated* when…

13. When the skiers saw that they were approaching a *fissure* in the glacier, they…

14. Captain Still knew that the engine room crew was *languid* from…

15. Using his *legerdemain*, the pickpocket…

## EXERCISE III—Roots, Prefixes, and Suffixes

*Study the entries and answer the questions that follow.*

The root *ver* means "true."
The root *fic* means "to do" or "to make."
The root *cra* means "to mix."
The root *sacr* means "sacred."
The root *idi* means "peculiar" or "one's own."
The prefix *e* means "completely."
The prefix *pro* means "in front of."
The suffix *fy* means "to make."
The prefix *suf* means "under."
The root *syn* means "together."

1. Using literal translations as guidance, define the following words without using a dictionary.

   A. verify          D. sacrifice
   B. very            E. idiom
   C. suffice         F. idiot

2. A *veracious* person will tell the _____ while under oath so that the jury can make a good _____ about the case.

3. Explain why the word *crater* contains a root that means "to mix." If you need a starting point, consider the physical shape of a crater.

4. Doing good deeds will be _____ to your community.

   If a machine can do its job with little fuel or wasted energy, then it is said to be _____.

   A[n] _____ worker can complete a job before any of the other workers.

## EXERCISE IV—Inference

*Complete the sentences by inferring information about the italicized word from its context.*

1. A *cessation* of fighting in the war-torn region allowed the residents...

2. The team asked the coach to *delineate* the complicated instructions because...

3. When Monica is in a hurry, she doesn't start conversations with her *garrulous* neighbor because...

## EXERCISE V—Writing

*Here is a writing prompt similar to the one you will find on the writing portion of the SAT.*

Plan and write an essay on the following statement:

> "Gratitude is when memory is stored in the heart and
> not in the mind."
> –Lionel Hampton

**Assignment**: Write an essay in which you explain Lionel Hampton's definition of gratitude. Support your points with evidence from your own reading, classroom studies, and personal observation and experience.

**Thesis**: Write a one-sentence response to the above statement. Make certain this single sentence offers a clear statement of your position.

*Example: What Lionel Hampton essentially means when he defines gratitude as "memory... stored in the heart and not the mind," is that gratitude is an irrational emotion, like love and loyalty, and not a rational thought process.*

**Organizational Plan:** If your thesis is the point on which you want to end, where does your essay need to begin? List the points of development that are inevitable in leading your reader from your beginning point to your end point. This is your outline.

**Draft:** Use your thesis as both your beginning and your end. Following your outline, write a good first draft of your essay. Remember to support all your points with examples, facts, references to reading, etc.

**Review and revise:** Exchange essays with a classmate. Using the scoring guide for Organization on page 240, score your partner's essay (while he or she scores yours). Focus on the organizational plan and the use of language conventions. If necessary, rewrite your essay to improve the organizational plan and/or your use of language.

## Improving Paragraphs

*Read the following passage and then answer the multiple-choice questions that follow. The questions will require you to make decisions regarding the revision of the reading selection.*

1     Few substances are as useful, beautiful, and plentiful as glass; it's practical and decorative uses are practically limitless. The ancient Mesopotamians discovered glass around 3500 B.C.E., when potters, who were making glazes for pottery, accidentally combined calciferous sand with soda ash. This early technique allowed them to make a variety of glass beads, seals, and plaques. Ornamental glass had been discovered.

2     The Roman Empire turned glass manufacturing into an industry by building furnaces that increased the production and quality of glass. By 100 C.E., Roman architects were incorporating glass windows in buildings. The glass was far from flawless and transparent like the glass of the present, but the windows did allow light into otherwise dark homes.

3     Before the Roman Empire, in 1500 B.C.E., Egyptian craftsmen covered compacted sand molds with molten glass in order to form the first glass vases. The craft quickly spread throughout Mesopotamia due to Egypt's influence through trade. In 27 B.C.E., Syrian artists discovered how to blow glass, which allowed them to craft a variety of glass shapes.

4     When the Roman Empire crumbled, the glass industry diversified. Geographic regions adopted their own unique methods and styles of glassmaking; southern regions, for example, used soda ash in production, while northern areas replaced soda ash with potash—an abundant material in the forested landscapes of the north.

5     Medieval architects further developed Roman glass by dyeing it different colors, and then combining the various colors of glass to form single windows. In the eleventh century, the multi-colored glass, or stained-glass windows, filled churches and palaces with exquisite light.

6     German glassmakers took glassmaking to the next step by cutting sheets from long cylinders of molten glass. The new type of glass became known as sheet glass, or crown glass. In the mid-seventeenth century, Venice lost its dominance in

glassmaking when the Englishman George Ravenscroft replaced potash with lead oxide and combined it with quartz sand. The combination produced highly reflective glass. Germans added lime to potash, which resulted in yet another variation of glass. Milch glass, as it is called, had the opaque white color of porcelain.

7 As the Middle Ages faded to the Renaissance, glassmaking guilds flourished, and many laws were created to protect each region's secret technique. At the time, Venice was the center of the industry, and the laws helped the city to maintain a monopoly on glass production; however, artists in cities such as Murano were experimenting with new mixtures of glass. Murano glassmakers replaced calciferous sand with quartz sand to produce a unique, crystal-like glass.

8 In 1688, France improved the production of plate glass. Used in mirrors. By pouring molten glass onto specially designed tables and then by polishing it with felt disks, French artisans created glass that could reflect images with little or no visual distortion. The newfound plate-glass technique resulted in the creation of the famous Hall of Mirrors in the Palace of Versailles. In the eighteenth century, cut glass became popular. Crystal-like in appearance and very reflective, cut glass was used for dishes and vases, as well as exquisite glass chandeliers.

9 The glass industry split at the end of the nineteenth century. Some artists followed the Art Nouveau style, in which designs mirrored elements of nature. The "new" artists saw their work as explorations of artistic expressions rather than mediums of practical application. Other artists embraced the new, efficient glassmaking methods that sprang from the industrial revolution, whereby bottles, jars, and plate glass could be produced by machines at a fraction of the cost of the hand-made items.

10 Today, the two divisions of glassmakers continue in the traditions of early glassmakers. New manufacturing techniques constantly increase the strength and versatility of glass, and artists continue to explore new styles that ensure glass is as pleasing to the eye as it is practical. The long history of glass, and its timeless use, ensures that it will exist for centuries to come.

1. Which of the following changes would fix a grammatical error in paragraph 1?
   A. Delete *B.C.E.*
   B. Spell *Mesopotamians* with a lower case *M*.
   C. Capitalize *potters*.
   D. Change *it's* to *its*.
   E. Delete the first sentence.

2. Which of the following changes in paragraph order would correct the chronology of the passage?
   A. 1, 2, 3, 4
   B. 1, 3, 2, 4
   C. 3, 1, 2, 4
   D. 1, 4, 2, 3
   E. 3, 4, 1, 2

3. Which of the following changes to paragraph 7 would improve the flow of the passage?
   A. Delete paragraph 7.
   B. Describe the location of Murano.
   C. Combine paragraph 7 with paragraph 8.
   D. Begin the passage with paragraph 7.
   E. Move paragraph 7 to follow paragraph 5.

4. Which of the following describes an error in paragraph 8?
   A. sentence fragment
   B. split infinitive
   C. cliché
   D. dangling modifier
   E. improper pronoun use

5. Paragraph 8 should not
   A. include a reference to the Hall of Mirrors because it is irrelevant to the subject.
   B. be included in the passage because it detracts from the topic.
   C. include the last two sentences because they belong in a separate paragraph.
   D. begin with a prepositional phrase because it is incorrect.
   E. fail to further explain the process of making cut glass.

# Lesson Twelve

1. **halcyon** (hal´ sē ən) *adj.* calm; pleasant
   The severe windstorm interrupted the otherwise *halcyon* week.
   *syn: tranquil; unruffled*　　　　　　　*ant: troubled; tumultuous*

2. **fastidious** (fa stid´ ē əs) *adj.* hard to please; fussy
   My neighbor is a *fastidious* housekeeper.
   *syn: meticulous; exacting*　　　　　　　*ant: casual; lax*

3. **badinage** (bad n äzh´) *n.* playful, teasing talk
   What began as *badinage* quickly escalated to cutting insults.
   *syn: chaff; joshing*

4. **malapropism** (mal´ ə prop iz´ m) *n.* a word humorously misused
   He used a *malapropism* when he said "conspire" in place of "inspire."

5. **garner** (gär´ nər) *v.* to gather; to acquire
   During the fall harvest, extra workers were hired to *garner* the crops.
   *syn: harvest*

6. **kismet** (kiz´ met) *n.* destiny; fate; fortune (one's lot in life)
   She thought her *kismet* was to be a veterinarian until she failed her biology lab.

7. **hegira** (hi jī´ rə) *n.* flight; escape
   The flooding caused a mass *hegira* from the city.

8. **paradigm** (par´ ə dīm) *n.* a model; an example
   The class regarded Kate as a *paradigm* of good manners.

9. **debauchery** (di bô´ chə rē) *n.* corruption; self-indulgence
   Sam was once wealthy, but a life of gambling and *debauchery* left him with nothing.
   *syn: excess; dissipation*

10. **milieu** (mēl yë´) *n.* environment; setting
    The poet felt that his proper *milieu* was the untouched wilderness of Alaska.

11. **regress** (ri gres´) *v.* to move backward
    If he took the job offer, Tim felt that his career might *regress* rather than move forward.

12. **bilious** (bil´ yəs) *adj.* bad tempered; cross
No one could stand being in the same room with Sam when he was in a *bilious* mood.
*syn: grouchy; cantankerous*           *ant: pleasant*

13. **necromancy** (nek´ rə man´ sē) *n.* magic, especially that practiced by a witch
Puritans often executed people who had supposedly practiced *necromancy*.
*syn: black magic; conjuring*

14. **gumption** (gump´ shən) *n.* courage and initiative; common sense
It takes a lot of *gumption* to succeed in this fast-paced society.
*syn: enterprise; aggressiveness; drive*

15. **blandishment** (blan´ dish mənt) *n.* flattery
The salesman's *blandishments* did not convince me to buy the expensive watch.
*syn: overpraise; bootlicking*

## EXERCISE I—Words in Context

*From the list below, supply the words needed to complete the paragraph. Some words will not be used.*

| | | | |
|---|---|---|---|
| bilious | milieu | hegira | halcyon |
| garner | paradigm | blandishment | malapropism |
| necromancy | fastidious | | |

1.  It took eight years for Megan to _____ the materials that she needed to make her front lawn the _____ of landscape design. Though she
is _____ about maintaining the lawn, she never allows herself to
become _____ when the neighbor's playful children accidentally
trample some of the flowers. The children always apologized, and the
younger girl's darling use of the _____ "scrubbers" instead of
"shrubs" made her far too adorable to scold.

    Deep down, Megan didn't care what people thought of her yard; she
didn't construct it to receive the _____ of other gardeners. Megan just
wanted a[n] _____ place in which she could relax or entertain guests.
She also thought that the natural _____ would inspire her writing.

    When Megan wasn't working on her verdant courtyard, she was typing
the manuscript for her first fantasy novel, a tale of sorcerers, goblins, and
_____.

*From the list below, supply the words needed to complete the paragraph. Some words will not be used.*

| | | | |
|---|---|---|---|
| gumption | debauchery | garner | regress |
| hegira | badinage | kismet | bilious |

2.  The quality of life in Omar's homeland _____ so much that people
ate roots to survive. The _____ of the crooked politicians in the former government had consumed any available relief funds. Fearing the
unpredictable warlords looting villages, Omar gathered his family and
joined the _____ from the war-torn region.

    The thought of a better life gave Omar the _____ to make the ardu-
ous trek with his wife and two children. The children faired well, despite
the harsh conditions of the journey; at night, the _____ between the
children revealed that their _____ of having to flee from a burning
homeland had not entirely ruined their childhood.

## EXERCISE II—Sentence Completion

*Complete the sentence in a way that shows you understand the meaning of the italicized vocabulary word.*

1. Bernard, who was once a penniless immigrant, used his *gumption* to...

2. Stanley did not send Phil to meet with the investors, because Phil's *bilious* manner might...

3. The writer moved out of the city after complaining that the urban *milieu* did not...

4. Molly was the *paradigm* of managers, so the executives...

5. Jimmy thought that football was his *kismet* in life until he...

6. When Bert used the *malapropism* "fire distinguisher" in place of "fire extinguisher," the English professor knew...

7. The *fastidious* youngster refused to eat unless the...

8. The salesperson at the expensive fashion shop used *blandishment* to...

9. The old witch used *necromancy* to...

10. Joe's condition *regressed* at the hospital because...

11. The rebels took over the island nation, but rampant *debauchery* in the new government caused...

12. Thousands of refugees made a *hegira* from their homeland because...

13. After the detective *garnered* enough evidence to place the suspect at the crime scene, she...

14. The bus driver was not easily distracted, but the *badinage* among the children...

15. Spending a day fishing on the *halcyon* lake would be a good way to...

**EXERCISE III—Roots, Prefixes, and Suffixes**

*Study the entries and answer the questions that follow.*

The root *greg* means "flock" or "herd."
The roots *val* and *vail* mean "to be strong" or "to be worthy."
The roots *ven*, *vent*, and *venu* mean "to come to" or "to approach."
The prefix *co* means "with" or "together."
The prefix *e* means "out" or "from."
The prefix *seg* means "apart."
The prefix *a* means "away" or "from."
The prefix *ambi* means "both" or "around."
The prefix *in* means "not."

1.  Using literal translations as guidance, define the following words without using a dictionary.

    A.  advent          D.  egregious
    B.  covenant        E.  invalid
    C.  ambivalent      F.  valiant

2.  If you come to exciting places, then you might be a[n] _____-seeker. The last day of your vacation will approach rapidly, so _____ you will have to go home, but not before you purchase a[n] _____ to remind you of the trip. If you didn't enjoy the trip, then you might explore different approaches, or _____, to your next getaway.

3.  _____ people enjoy the company of others; they often congregate on the weekend for dinner or conversation.

    Concrete mixed with rocks is a[n] _____ solution because you could break it up and _____ the rocks from the concrete if you wanted to.

4.  The brave soldier received a medal for _____ in combat after his batallion _____ over the enemy forces.

## EXERCISE IV—Inference

*Complete the sentences by inferring information about the italicized word from its context.*

1. Autumn needed to *garner* information about her family's history, and she began the task by…

2. Brianna feels that her *kismet* in life is to be a doctor, so she is going to…

3. When Jared leaves empty pizza boxes on the living room floor, his *fastidious* roommate…

## EXERCISE V—Critical Reading

*Below is a pair of reading passages followed by several multiple-choice questions similar to the ones you will encounter on the SAT. Carefully read both passages and choose the best answer to each of the questions.*

*The first passage, adapted from English writer-philosopher John Stuart Mill's 1859 essay "On Liberty," emphasizes the importance of individuality among tyrannical majorities.*

*The second passage, from 1776, is an excerpt from Adam Smith's book, <u>The Wealth of Nations</u>. Adam Smith's philosophies helped to inspire the creation of America's free-market capitalist economy. In this passage, the Scottish philosopher explains that the division of labor is a product of self-interest—the natural force that drives all human activity.*

### Passage 1

In sober truth, whatever homage may be professed, or even paid, to real or supposed mental superiority, the general tendency of things throughout the world is to render mediocrity the ascendant power among mankind. In ancient history, in the middle ages, and in a diminishing degree through the long transition from feudali-
5  ty to the present time, the individual was power in himself; and if he had either great talents or a high social position, he was a considerable power. At present, individuals are lost in the crowd. In politics, it is almost a triviality to say that public opinion now rules the world. The only power deserving the name is that of masses, and of governments while they make themselves the organ of the tendencies and
10  instincts of masses. This is as true in the moral and social relations of private life as

in public transactions. Those whose opinions go by the name of public opinion, are not always the same sort of public: in America, they are the whole white population; in England, chiefly the middle class. But they are always a mass, that is to say, collective mediocrity. And what is still greater novelty, the mass do not now take
15 their opinions from dignitaries in Church or State, from ostensible leaders, or from books. Their thinking is done for them by men much like themselves, addressing them or speaking in their name, on the spur of the moment, through the newspapers. I am not complaining of all this. I do not assert that anything better is compatible, as a general rule, with the present low state of the human mind. But that
20 does not hinder the government of mediocrity from being mediocre government. No government by a democracy or a numerous aristocracy, either in its political acts or in the opinions, qualities, and tone of mind which it fosters, ever did or could rise above mediocrity, except in so far as the sovereign Many have let themselves be
25 guided (which in their best times they always have done) by the counsels and influence of a more highly gifted and instructed One or Few. The initiation of all wise or noble things, comes and must come from individuals; generally at first from some one individual. The honor and glory of the average man is that he is capable of following that initiative; that he can respond internally to wise and noble things,
30 and be led to them with his eyes open. I am not countenancing the sort of "hero-worship" which applauds the strong man of genius for forcibly seizing on the government of the world and making it do his bidding in spite of itself. All he can claim is freedom to point out the way. The power of compelling others into it, is not only inconsistent with the freedom and development of all the rest, but corrupting to the
35 strong man himself. It does seem, however, that when the opinions of masses of merely average men are everywhere become or becoming the dominant power, the counterpoise and corrective to that tendency would be the more and more pronounced individuality of those who stand on the higher eminences of thought. It is in these circumstances most especially that exceptional individuals, instead of
40 being deterred, should be encouraged in acting differently from the mass. In other times there was no advantage in their doing so, unless they acted not only differently, but better. In this age, the mere example of non-conformity, the mere refusal to bend the knee to custom, is itself a service. Precisely because the tyranny of opinion is such as to make eccentricity a reproach, it is desirable, in order to break
45 through that tyranny, that people should be eccentric. Eccentricity has always abounded when and where strength of character has abounded; and the amount of eccentricity in a society has generally been proportional to the amount of genius, mental vigor, and moral courage which it contained. That so few now dare to be eccentric marks the chief danger of the time.

## Passage 2

Division of labor, from which so many advantages are derived, is not originally the effect of any human wisdom which foresees and intends that general opulence to which it gives occasion. It is the necessary, though very slow and gradual, consequence of a certain propensity in human nature…to truck, barter and exchange one thing for another.

In almost every other race of animals, each individual animal, when it is grown up to maturity, is entirely independent, and in its natural state has the occasion for the assistance of no other living creature.

But man has almost constant occasion for the help of his brethren, and it is in vain for him to expect it from their benevolence only. He will be more likely to prevail if he can interest their self-love in his favor and show them that it is for their own advantage to do for him what he requires of them.

It is not from the benevolence of the butcher, the brewer or the baker that we expect our dinner, but from their regard to their own interest. We address ourselves not to their humanity, but to their self-love, and never talk to them of our own necessities, but of their advantages.

As it is by treaty, by barter, and by purchase that we obtain from one another the greater part of those mutual good offices which we stand in need of, so it is this same trucking disposition which originally gives occasion to the division of labor. In a tribe of hunters or shepherds, a particular person makes bows and arrows, for example, with more readiness and dexterity than any other. He frequently exchanges them for cattle or venison with his companions; and he finds at last that he can in this manner get more cattle and venison than if he himself went to the field to catch them.

From a regard to his own interest, therefore, the making of bows and arrows grows to be his chief business, and he becomes a sort of armorer. Another excels in making the frames and covers of their little huts or movable houses. He is accustomed to be of use in this way to his neighbors, who reward him in the same manner with cattle and venison, till at last he finds it his interest to dedicate himself entirely to this employment, to become a sort of house carpenter. In the same manner a third becomes a smith or a brazier; a fourth, a tanner or dresser of hides or skins.

And thus, the certainty of being able to exchange all that surplus part of the produce of his own labor, which is over and above his own consumption, for such parts of the produce of other men's labor as he may have occasion for, encourages every man to apply himself to a particular occupation, and to cultivate and bring to perfection whatever talent or genius he may possess for that particular species of business.

1. As used throughout the first passage, *mediocrity* most nearly means
   A. of no exceptional quality.
   B. out-of-tune.
   C. of a boring nature.
   D. unintelligent.
   E. of no origin.

2. According to the first passage, it is inevitable that people will
   A. allow democratic governments to turn socialist.
   B. elect intelligent, independent, government representatives.
   C. allow themselves to be imprisoned.
   D. allow themselves to be governed by mediocre people making dull decisions.
   E. make inane decisions about their own futures.

3. The author of the first passage probably believes that
   A. people should avoid any form of government.
   B. the government should consist of two or three people at most.
   C. the decision of one wise individual is preferable to a decision made by a group of ordinary people.
   D. it is unethical to produce so much of a product that there is a surplus.
   E. wise individuals generally make better decisions than groups of wise individuals, but if the group gets too big, it makes mediocre decisions.

4. According to passage 1, the *honor and glory of the average man* is
   A. his ability to follow his own wise and noble ideas.
   B. continuing to exist by getting his name in the history books.
   C. his readiness to accept public opinion.
   D. his penchant for intelligent conversation.
   E. his many technological achievements through hard work.

5. *Division of labor* probably refers to
   A. the shortening of the work week to forty hours.
   B. separating men and women in the workplace.
   C. individuals choosing careers based on their own needs or talents.
   D. ensuring that workers can do any job in a manufacturing process.
   E. the effects that labor unions have on industry.

6. As used in lines 4 and 19 of passage 2, the terms *truck* and *trucking* probably refer to
   A. shipping goods.
   B. insider trading.
   C. using oxcarts to move goods.
   D. farming.
   E. bartering.

7. Which of the following choices best paraphrases the following sentence?

   > It is not from the benevolence of the butcher, the brewer or the baker that we expect our dinner, but from their regard to their own interest.

   A. In 1776, there are no good people in the services industry.
   B. Butchers, bakers, and brewers do not provide their services to us out of the goodness of their own hearts; they do it to help themselves.
   C. Be careful when you shop for food, because butchers and bakers just want to make money, so they'll sell you anything.
   D. Butchers, bakers, and brewers are not really slaves, because they enjoy what they are doing.
   E. Good blue-collar workers drive the success of a free economy.

8. The author of passage 2 suggests that workers should have specific jobs because
   A. some people cannot perform certain tasks.
   B. the psychological implications of never learning how to do a good job at one thing would lead to failed businesses and broken families.
   C. they want raises whenever they have to learn new things.
   D. workers in general are not intelligent enough to be good at five or six different jobs.
   E. workers will perfect their skills at specific jobs, which benefits everyone.

9. Passage 2 includes the example of commerce in a primitive tribe because
   A. it supports the author's assertion that bartering is a product of human nature.
   B. it supports the author's assertion that the division of labor is a natural human tendency.
   C. it supports the idea that mankind will never change in behavior.
   D. the example provides comic relief to the passage.
   E. primitive tribes were very proficient at manufacturing.

10. Which of the following choices best describes the difference in intent between the passages?
   A. The author of the first passage identifies a problem and responds to it, while the author of the second passage simply explains a theory.
   B. The first passage is written in third-person point of view, while the second passage is in first-person.
   C. The passages have opposite topics.
   D. The first passage uses no examples in support of its topic.
   E. Only the first passage suggests the importance of the individual.

11. Both of the passages were written before
   A. the United States was colonized.
   B. the twentieth century.
   C. tribes learned how to make bows and arrows.
   D. America was discovered.
   E. newspapers were invented.

12. Which of the following best describes the difference in tone between the passages?
   A. Passage 2 is more condemning than passage 1.
   B. Passage 1 is entirely positive, and passage 2 is negative.
   C. Neither of the passages has a title.
   D. Passage 1 is mildly disparaging, while passage 2 is constructive.
   E. Passage 1 is about government, while passage 2 is about economy.

# Lesson Thirteen

1. **nirvana** (nər vä´ nə) *n.* a condition of great peace or happiness
After work, Irene sought *nirvana* through meditation.

2. **salutary** (sal´ yə ter ē) *adj.* healthful; wholesome
The country air had a *salutary* influence on the child's chronic cough.
*syn: beneficial*             *ant: pernicious*

3. **despicable** (des´ pi kə bəl) *adj.* contemptible; hateful
Only a *despicable* cad would behave so horribly.
*syn: vile; base*           *ant: laudable; worthy*

4. **harlequin** (här´ lə kwən) *n.* a clown
The king summoned the *harlequin* to entertain the dinner guests.

5. **empathy** (em´ pə thē) *n.* an understanding of another's feelings
The same thing happened to me once, so I felt *empathy* for the person whose car broke down on the interstate.
*syn: appreciation; compassion*

6. **brevity** (brev´ i tē) *n.* briefness; short duration
The *brevity* of the candidate's speech surprised everyone.
*syn: terseness; conciseness*       *ant: lengthiness*

7. **savant** (sə vänt´) *n.* a person of extensive learning; an eminent scholar
Einstein was a *savant* who will always be remembered for $E = MC^2$.

8. **obsequious** (əb sē´ kwē əs) *adj.* excessively submissive or overly attentive
The waiter's *obsequious* behavior annoyed the patrons at the expensive restaurant.
*syn: servile; fawning*       *ant: domineering; haughty*

9. **redundant** (ri dun´ dant) *adj.* repetitious; using more words than needed
Saying that a person is a rich millionaire is *redundant*.
*syn: wordy; excessive; unnecessary*     *ant: essential*

10. **offal** (ô´ fəl) *n.* garbage; waste parts
No one wanted the task of carrying the *offal* from the butcher shop to the trash container.

11. **hoi polloi** (hoi´ pə loi´ ) *n.* the common people; the masses
The *hoi polloi* loved to watch the Christians fight the lions.

12. **sentient** (sen´ shənt) *adj.* conscious; capable of feeling or perceiving
No one knew if the girl in the coma was *sentient,* but they continued to hold and talk to her.
*syn: alert; alive; cognizant*

13. **impinge** (im pinj´) *v.* to encroach; to trespass
Do not *impinge* on your neighbors by walking in uninvited.
*syn: infringe; intrude*

14. **cataract** (kat´ ə rakt) *n.* a large waterfall
Because of the *cataract* in that part of the river, you can't put a canoe in the water.

15. **animosity** (an ə mos´ i tē) *n.* hatred
There was more *animosity* between the opposing teams' fans than between the teams themselves.
*syn: ill-will; hostility*                     *ant: friendliness; congeniality*

## EXERCISE I—Words in Context

*From the list below, supply the words needed to complete the paragraph. Some words will not be used.*

| | | | |
|---|---|---|---|
| cataract | harlequin | hoi polloi | salutary |
| nirvana | empathy | animosity | |

1.   Paul was never very sociable, so when he tired of the _____ of the city, he sought _____ in the peace of the wilderness. At least once a week, he took a[n] _____ hike on the trail behind his house until he reached Toby Creek. A drastic change in elevation there created a sparkling _____, and the noise of the falling water seemed to flush away any _____ that Paul had generated during the workday.

From the list below, supply the words needed to complete the paragraph. Some words will not be used.

| | | | |
|---|---|---|---|
| obsequious | cataract | brevity | savant |
| harlequin | empathy | despicable | offal |

2.    The _____ ruler had no _____ for the citizens who could not afford to pay higher taxes; she ordered them to be imprisoned. Fearing the queen's wrath, the servants responded to her every wish in a[n] _____ manner. The _____ dreaded entertaining her, because he feared that his wit might offend her. Though the queen was a self-proclaimed _____, most of the jester's jokes went right over her head. The _____ of her reign can be attributed to her assassination.

From the list below, supply the words needed to complete the paragraph. Some words will not be used.

| | | |
|---|---|---|
| hoi polloi | redundant | offal |
| savant | impinge | sentient |

3.    Barely _____ after working a twelve-hour shift at the seafood processing plant, Sal used the forklift to move drums of fish _____ reserved for fisherman to use as chum. The task was nearly finished, but Sal felt work was _____ on his family life, and he spilled four hundred gallons of rotting fish parts onto the loading dock. Sal didn't know what would be worse: cleaning up the disgusting mess or enduring another _____ lecture from his boss about losing concentration.

## EXERCISE II—Sentence Completion

*Complete the sentence in a way that shows you understand the meaning of the italicized vocabulary word.*

1. The war was long over, but the *animosity* between the two nations still caused…

2. Shawna had just finished working a double shift at the plant, so she felt as if she had reached *nirvana* when she finally…

3. The rafters began drifting toward the *cataract* in the river ahead, so they…

4. Flash cards and practice problems are *salutary* ways for students to…

5. Many thought that the new seatbelt law *impinged* their…

6. The *despicable* pirate forced the prisoners to…

7. The crash victim was *sentient*, but she could not…

8. The *harlequin* danced and juggled batons in an attempt to…

9. The *hoi polloi* did not really notice the new legislation until…

10. Logan, who knew what it was like to lose friends, expressed his *empathy* for Kim during…

11. The pig farmer used the *offal* from the dinner table to…

12. The audience members appreciated the *brevity* of the professor's conclusion, because they…

13. When Kyle's parents noticed his *obsequious* behavior, they knew that…

14. The *savant* impressed everyone with her ability to…

15. The editor fixed the *redundant* sentence by…

## EXERCISE III—Roots, Prefixes, and Suffixes

*Study the entries and answer the questions that follow.*

The root *anim* means "feeling," "spirit," or "life."
The roots *sec* and *sect* mean "cut."
The root *cand* means "to shine."
The suffix *id* means "tending to."
The root *magn* means "great."
The root *un* means "one."
The root *ence* means "of."

1.  Using literal translations as guidance, define the following words without using a dictionary.

    A.  reanimate          D.  candescence
    B.  magnanimous        E.  intersect
    C.  candidate          F.  bisect

2.  The literal meaning of *unanimous* is _____.

    There is _____ between two people who dislike each other, but *animation* is the act of _____.

3.  An *incandescent* light bulb is _____, but the word *candid* comes from the same root and it means *pure* or *sincere*. Describe the probable evolution of the word *candid*.

4.  List as many words as you can think of that contain the root *sect*.

5.  List as many words as you can think of that contain the root *anim*.

## EXERCISE IV—Inference

*Complete the sentences by inferring information about the italicized word from its context.*

1.  Max knew that the clothing shop was hurting for business, because the *obsequious* salesman would not...

2.  The *redundant* phrase, "2:00 a.m. in the morning," should be rewritten to omit "in the morning" because...

3.  Charlie had genuine *empathy* for the troubled youths because he, too, had grown up in...

## EXERCISE V—Writing

*Here is a writing prompt similar to the one you will find on the writing portion of the SAT.*

Plan and write an essay based on the following statement:

> We shall never understand the natural environment until we see it as being an organism. Land can be healthy or sick, fertile or barren, rich or poor, lovingly nurtured or bled white. Our present attitudes and laws governing the ownership and use of land represent an abuse of the concept of private property.
>
> Today you can murder land for private profit. You can leave the corpse for all to see and nobody calls the cops.
>
> –A quotation from *The Pursuit of Wilderness*, by Paul Brooks, 1971.

**Assignment:** In a well-organized essay, refute or defend the excerpt. Support your position by discussing examples from current events, classroom studies, science, technology, or your own personal observations and experience.

**Thesis:** Write a one-sentence response to the above assignment. Make certain this single sentence offers a clear statement of your position.

*Example: While his observation that the natural environment is like a living organism is accurate enough, Paul Brooks is overdramatic in his assessment of our current laws regarding the use and protection of the world's resources and habitats.*

**Organizational Plan:** If your thesis is the point on which you want to end, where does your essay need to begin? List the points of development that are inevitable in leading your reader from your beginning point to your end point. This list is your outline.

**Draft:** Use your thesis as both your beginning and your end. Following your outline, write a good first draft of your essay. Remember to support all your points with examples, facts, references to reading, etc.

**Review and revise:** Exchange essays with a classmate. Using the scoring guide for Development on page 241, score your partner's essay (while he or she scores yours). Focus on the development of ideas and the use of language conventions. If necessary, rewrite your essay to improve the development of ideas and/or your use of language.

## Identifying Sentence Errors

*Identify the grammatical error in each of the following sentences. If the sentence contains no error, select answer choice E.*

1. Uninterested students <u>commonly exhibit</u> one or more of the following
   (A)
   <u>symptoms:</u> withdrawal, <u>rebelliousness</u>, restlessness, and <u>they are tired.</u>
    (B)                        (C)                           (D)
   <u>No error</u>
    (E)

2. I did not enjoy <u>speech class</u> today <u>because</u> my teacher was very
                     (A)           (B)
   <u>critical to my</u> <u>presentation.</u>   <u>No error</u>
      (C)       (D)      (E)

3. <u>Generalizing</u> is <u>easier than</u> <u>grounding</u> one's thoughts <u>in reality.</u>
    (A)          (B)     (C)                  (D)
   <u>No error</u>
    (E)

4. The <u>politician</u> declared, "I <u>promise that</u> <u>I will never</u> <u>except a bribe!"</u>
       (A)                (B)        (C)     (D)
   <u>No error</u>
    (E)

5. <u>Today in America,</u> <u>there seems to be</u> nothing more important <u>than</u> being
       (A)         (B)                            (C)
   rich, looking good, and <u>to have a good time.</u>   <u>No error</u>
                        (D)        (E)

## Improving Sentences

*The underlined portion of each sentence below contains some flaw. Select the answer choice that best corrects the flaw.*

6. <u>Ringing loudly, John reached over his head and hit the alarm clock.</u>
   A. Ringing loudly, the alarm clock was reached over John's head.
   B. John reached over his head and hit the alarm clock, ringing loudly.
   C. John reached over his head and hit the loudly ringing alarm clock.
   D. The alarm clock, ringing loudly, was reached by John over his head.
   E. John, ringing loudly, hit the clock over his head.

7. When Pratt rushed into the cottage, he was <u>as white as a ghost and it was crystal clear that he had been playing with fire when he fed the wild animal.</u>
   A. pale with fear, and it was obvious that he had taken a risk when he fed the wild animal.
   B. as white as a ghost, making it crystal clear that he should not have played with fire by feeding a wild animal.
   C. terrified because it was crystal clear that the wild animal was playing with fire.
   D. white as a ghost when the wild animal made it crystal clear not to play with fire.
   E. crystal clear by the wild animal's ghostly appearance by the fire.

8. Today's politicians frequently give speeches about <u>problems concerning the environment and world peace with terrorism.</u>
   A. pollution, exploration, and terrorism.
   B. pollution, acid rain, and terrorism.
   C. problems in the news.
   D. problems they have a personal interest in.
   E. famine and arms control.

9.  <u>The cat lay quite motionless in front of the cupboard. Waiting silently for</u>
    <u>the mouse to emerge.</u>
    A.  The cat was lying quite motionless in front of the cupboard, waiting
        silently for the mouse to emerge.
    B.  The cat lay, quite motionless, in front of the cupboard. Waiting
        silently for the mouse to emerge.
    C.  The cat lay quite motionless in front of the cupboard. Waiting
        silently for the mouse to come out.
    D.  Waiting silently for the mouse to emerge, the cat lay quite motionless
        in front of the cupboard.
    E.  The cat was lying quite motionless in front of the cupboard. Waiting
        silently for the mouse to emerge.

10. <u>The rock concert was the most bizarre event I have ever witnessed.</u>
    <u>Especially since the lead guitarist destroyed his most priceless guitar as part</u>
    <u>of the show.</u>
    A.  The rock concert was the most bizarre event I have ever witnessed,
        especially since the lead guitarist destroyed his most priceless guitar as
        part of the show.
    B.  The rock concert was a bizarre event. The lead guitarist destroyed his
        priceless guitar as part of the show.
    C.  The rock concert was a bizarre event since the lead guitarist destroyed
        his very priceless guitar as part of the show.
    D.  The rock concert was the most bizarre event I have ever witnessed,
        especially since the lead guitarist destroyed his priceless guitar as part
        of the show.
    E.  The rock concert was an event I had never witnessed especially since
        the lead guitarist destroyed his most priceless guitar as part of the show.

# Lesson Fourteen

1. **bombast** (bom´ bast) *n.* impressive but meaningless language
Please, professor, spare the *bombast*; just give me the facts.

2. **orthography** (ôr thog´ rə fē) *n.* correct spelling
Anne's excellent spelling grades are testament to her grasp of *orthography.*

3. **paleontology** (pā lē ən tol´ ə jē) *n.* a science dealing with prehistoric life through the study of fossils
The expert in *paleontology* dated the skeleton to 2000 B.C.

4. **recoil** (ri koil´) *v.* to retreat; to draw back
Liz *recoiled* from the harsh words as though she had been struck.

5. **panache** (pə nash´) *n.* self-confidence; a showy manner
The actor always exhibited great *panache,* so his first appearance on the talk show didn't make him the least bit nervous.
*syn: charisma; spirit*

6. **saturnine** (sat´ er nīn) *adj.* gloomy; sluggish
The hostess' *saturnine* attitude caused the party to end early.
*syn: sullen; morose*          *ant: genial*

7. **endemic** (en dem´ ik) *adj.* confined to a particular country or area
Once it had been *endemic* to Africa, but now it is becoming a world-wide epidemic.
*syn: native; indigenous*          *ant: alien; foreign*

8. **mendacious** (men dā´ shəs) *adj.* lying; false; deceitful
Everyone knew the politician was *mendacious,* yet the voters kept reelecting him.
*syn: duplicitous*          *ant: truthful*

9. **obviate** (ob´ vē āt) *v.* to prevent; to get around
They delayed the release of the film in order to *obviate* a barrage of criticism.
*syn: circumvent*

10. **paroxysm** (par´ ək siz əm) *n.* a sudden outburst; a fit
The class, in a *paroxysm* of laughter, went silent as soon as the principal walked into the room.
*syn: outburst; commotion*

11. **aggrandize**   (ə gran´ dīz)   v.   1. to increase the range of; to expand   2. to make appear larger
    Much of what they did was not intended to aid their country, but to *aggrandize* their own positions.
    The advertisement *aggrandizes* the new product by making it appear as though everyone owns one.
    (1) *syn: enlarge; augment; enrich*          *ant: decrease; diminish*
    (2) *syn: exaggerate; embellish*          *ant: belittle; devalue*

12. **deign**   (dān)   v.   to lower oneself before an inferior
    "After what she did to me, I would not *deign* to say hello to her," said Mary about her former best friend.
    *syn: stoop; condescend*

13. **flaunt**   (flônt)   v.   to show off
    Some people *flaunt* their wealth by buying islands.
    *syn: boast; exhibit*          *ant: conceal*

14. **shibboleth**   (shib´ ə lith)   n.   a word or pronunciation that distinguishes someone as of a particular group
    Pronouncing "creek" as "crick" is a *shibboleth* of people in mid-Atlantic states.

15. **elicit**   (i lis´ it)   v.   to draw forth; to call forth
    The attorney tried to *elicit* a response from his client, but the man remained silent.
    *syn: evoke; extract*          *ant: cover; suppress*

## EXERCISE I—Words in Context

*From the list below, supply the words needed to complete the paragraph. Some words will not be used.*

| | | | |
|---|---|---|---|
| recoil | bombast | paleontology | panache |
| flaunt | elicit | shibboleth | aggrandize |
| obviate | endemic | | |

1.  When Dr. Carter is not fulfilling his duties as the professor of _____ at Ganton College, he is in the jungles of South America supervising excavations of ancient creatures. During the last dig, Dr. Carter _____ when a poisonous snake tried to bite him. Now he wears tall boots and gloves to _____ the risk of dangerous animals _____ to the region. He will definitely _____ the need for such safety measures. Some of the incoming scientists will accuse him of self-_____, despite the fact that the sociable doctor always avoids using too much _____ when speaking about safety; he'll _____ his findings when he returns to the campus at the end of the summer. He can put his _____ to better use in the classroom.

*From the list below, supply the words needed to complete the paragraph. Some words will not be used.*

| | | | |
|---|---|---|---|
| shibboleth | obviate | mendacious | deign |
| orthography | saturnine | paroxysm | endemic |

2.  Baker _____ to nod to his Nazi captors, and he immediately suffered the consequences. Without looking, Baker listened to the _____ of his cellmates. "What was that? What, are you working for them, too?"

   He understood their paranoia. Just weeks before, a[n] _____ rebel captive had revealed the escape plan to the guards. The prisoners, including Baker, had to abandon months of secrecy and labor that went into the construction of the tunnel. They had not yet regrouped; most of the _____ prisoners simply lay in their cells, defeated.

   Baker sat against the wall and thought about his capture. He had misused the _____ that the Nazis used to identify foreign spies, and the lack of _____ on his forged travel documents instantly signaled that he was not the German officer he claimed to have been. They must need information, he reasoned, or they would have executed him by now.

## EXERCISE II—Sentence Completion

*Complete the sentence in a way that shows you understand the meaning of the italicized vocabulary word.*

1.  The *mendacious* thief used forged credentials to...

2.  The *endemic* species of squirrel is only found in...

3.  To *obviate* a surprise attack, the lieutenant sent a scout ahead to...

4.  The *saturnine* children just stared out the window and said that they...

5.  If you show too much *panache* at the interview, you might...

6.  The queen *aggrandized* her power and influence by...

7.  Bill *recoiled* when he saw that the person on the news broadcast was...

8.  Helen promised that if Kelly had another *paroxysm* when she heard the word "no," Helen would...

9.  The *paleontology* class visited the museum to observe the...

10. The duke was not well-liked among his subjects because he never *deigned* to...

11. Attention to *orthography* is especially important on your college application because...

12. Charlie worked for thirty years to buy his Corvette, and he *flaunted* it by...

13. Save your *bombast* for the presentation and just give us the...

14. The suspicious soldier at the entry gate misspoke the *shibboleth*, so the guard refused to...

15. What she did was wrong, but it should not *elicit* the...

## EXERCISE III—Roots, Prefixes, and Suffixes

*Study the entries, and answer the questions that follow.*

The root *mon* means "to advise," "to remind," or "to warn."
The roots *volv* and *volut* mean "to roll" or "to turn."
The root *ambulare* means "to walk."
The suffix *ance* means "state of" or "quality of."
The prefix *per* means "through" or "completely."
The prefix *e* means "from" or "out."
The prefix *de* means "down" or "thoroughly."

1.  Using literal translations as guidance, define the following words without using a dictionary.

    A.  revolve
    B.  devolve
    C.  evolve

    D.  premonition
    E.  monster
    F.  demonstrate

2.  A[n] _____ might remind you that you should be in class, and an *admonishment* should _____ you to improve your behavior.

3.  If an injured person cannot walk, then he might need a[n] _____ to transport him to a doctor. If you *perambulate* a tunnel, then you _____ it.

4.  A *volume* is a collection of documents. Using what you know about the history of paper, explain why *volume*, which uses the root *vol*, "to roll," came to mean "a collection of documents."

## EXERCISE IV—Inference

*Complete the sentences by inferring information about the italicized word from its context.*

1.  The owners of the store had record profits, so they plan to *aggrandize* their share of the market even more by...

2.  The amnesia victim had no memory of his identity, so a hypnotist tried to *elicit* clues from the man's subconscious that...

3.  On the raft, Irene *obviated* the danger of drowning by...

## EXERCISE V—Critical Reading

*Below is a reading passage followed by several multiple-choice questions similar to the ones you will encounter on your SAT. Carefully read the passage and choose the best answer to each of the questions.*

*The following article details the exploits of the obscure Joshua Norton—a bankrupted businessman who, in 1859, declared himself Emperor of the United States. The city of San Francisco humored the eccentric Norton, and for twenty-one years, he "ruled" the United States, sometimes with the assistance of his two dogs: Bummer and Lazarus.*

America's short history is so full of interesting characters that some of them naturally get overlooked—even rulers as prestigious as Norton I, Emperor of the United States and Protector of Mexico.

Joshua Norton was born an Englishman around the year 1819, but his family
5    soon moved to South Africa and grew wealthy as traders. By the time Norton turned thirty, news of gold discoveries in California had spread around the world, and Norton, like many young entrepreneurs, relocated to San Francisco hoping to make his fortune in the rapidly growing city. Norton had quite a running start, too; he arrived in San Francisco with forty-thousand dollars in hand.
10    Norton did not find riches in gold, but he did find wealth in rice. The large population of Chinese immigrants in San Francisco ensured a high demand for the grain, and in four years, Norton had banked nearly one-quarter million dollars. When a famine in China caused the price of rice to skyrocket, Norton cleverly decided to multiply his money by purchasing all of the rice in the city; unfortunate-
15    ly, immediately after Norton spent his last penny acquiring what he thought was the only ship of rice in the city, many more ships arrived—all loaded with rice. The cost of rice plunged well below what it had been before the famine, and Norton was financially ruined.

Norton spent the next three years in court trying to recoup his losses and retain
20    his property. He lost every case, and the trauma took a toll on Norton's wit. He vanished for a year, and then, in 1857, Norton returned as a different man, apparently obsessed with the bureaucratic inadequacies of the nation; however, no one knew just how obsessed Norton had become.

In the year 1859, Joshua Norton proclaimed himself Norton I, Emperor of the
25    United States. A San Francisco newspaper printed the very formal decree, which also summoned representatives of all states to assemble at a San Francisco music hall to discuss the Emperor's modifications to national legislation; however, the latter never occurred because Norton decided to abolish the United States Congress before the meeting day arrived.
30    Angered by the rebellious government's unwillingness to desist operations, Norton issued another decree, this time ordering the commanding general of the United States Army, by name, to assemble a force and "clear the Halls of Congress." Strangely, neither Congress nor General Scott responded to the Emperor's demand,

so in 1860, Norton used his imperial authority to disband the Union entirely. Along
35    the way, the Emperor also assumed the duty of Protector of Mexico, but he retained
the position for only a decade before deciding that not even an Emperor as clever
as Norton was capable of protecting Mexico.

During his reign, the regal Norton forewent the traditional minutiae of emperors
in order to be close to his many beloved subjects. Each day he marched, sans
40    entourage, though the streets of San Francisco, inspecting the many properties and
processes of his capital city. Citizens recognized him immediately, for each day he
wore the Emperor's regalia: a blue military uniform complete with gold epaulets, a
beaver hat with a feather plume, and a battered sword. Sometimes Norton simply
enlightened his subjects on matters of state, and, on at least one occasion, the wise
45    Emperor was known to have intervened in order to quell a riot.

For most of his reign, Emperor Norton retired each night in the imperial suite of
his estate—a barren, closet-sized room in a boardinghouse; however, Norton's spar-
tan accommodations did not reflect the services that his loyal subjects provided for
him. During the reign of Norton, all established eateries welcomed the Emperor to
50    partake of complimentary dinners and lunches. Theaters and music halls reserved
seats for the sovereign, and public officials often acknowledged their benevolent
ruler.

Occasionally, matters of such importance would arise that Norton was compelled
to issue more edicts, and the major city newspapers were more than happy to
55    humor the Emperor. The Civil War (1861–1865) was of great concern to Norton,
and he issued several decrees addressing the violent conflict. Other edicts dealt with
matters of diplomacy or responded to various injustices of Norton's concern. In an
effort to resolve political skirmishes, Norton, in 1869, officially eliminated both the
Democratic and Republican parties. Three years later, he outlawed the word
60    "Frisco," because it "has no linguistic or other warrant," according to the official
decree. Violators of the "High Misdemeanor" were to pay a fine of twenty-five dollars.

The reign of Emperor Norton I lasted until January 8th, 1880, when the kindly
monarch collapsed during his daily duties. People immediately reacted to save the
65    aging sovereign, but no one could help. The newspaper headlines on the following
day read "Le Roi est Mort"—"the king is dead."

The good Emperor left an estate valued at approximately ten dollars, but more
importantly, he left a priceless impression on his many subjects. An estimated ten
thousand people lined the streets in order to pay homage to their fallen monarch
70    during the funeral, and the City of San Francisco paid for Norton's burial. Norton
is now at peace, but his story will live on in the imaginations of anyone who hap-
pens to catch a glimpse of an old photograph portraying the bizarre but munificent
Norton the First.

1. Emperor Norton I was born in
   A. South Africa.
   B. San Francisco.
   C. England.
   D. Germany.
   E. Mexico.

2. Joshua Norton lost his fortune because
   A. he was never a competent businessman.
   B. he spent all of his money on rice, and then the price of rice plunged.
   C. in his madness, he forgot the location of his assets.
   D. he bought a cargo ship, and then the bank foreclosed on him.
   E. he had to pay tribute to the State of California for his title.

3. In which year did Norton lose his fortune?
   A. 1849
   B. 1851
   C. 1853
   D. 1857
   E. 1859

4. As used in line 20, *wit* most nearly means
   A. perspective.
   B. behavior.
   C. neurotic.
   D. judgment.
   E. sanity.

5. In 1860, the commanding general of the U.S. Army was
   A. Scott.
   B. Macarthur.
   C. Patton.
   D. Byron.
   E. Norton.

6. As used in line 38, *traditional minutiae* probably refers to
   A. diplomatic influence.
   B. time limits for meeting with subjects.
   C. punishing rebels of the empire.
   D. wealth and luxuries.
   E. uniform and apparel.

7. Which of the following was *not* a detail in one of Norton's imperial orders?
   A. summoning state representatives to meet in Reno
   B. abolishing two major political parties
   C. removing Congress with military force
   D. prohibiting the use of the word *Frisco*
   E. dissolving the Union

8. The tone of this passage is best described as
   A. sullen and bitter.
   B. farcical but respectful.
   C. overbearing but impersonal.
   D. churlish and vexing.
   E. distant but delicate.

9. The primary purpose of this passage is to
   A. persuade readers to vacation in San Francisco.
   B. explain the symptoms of obsessive-compulsive disorder.
   C. entertain readers with Norton's exploits.
   D. inform about an interesting character in American history.
   E. inform readers of the pandemonium surrounding the gold rush.

10. According to the passage, the people of San Francisco regard Norton as
    A. a respected leader who turned misfortune into success.
    B. an important lesson in investment risks and overworking.
    C. a harmless but entertaining delusional man and pillar of the community.
    D. a justification to pursue the science of psychology.
    E. their honorary Governor of California.

# REVIEW

## Lessons 8 – 14

### EXERCISE I – Sentence Completion

*Choose the best pair of words to complete the sentence. Most choices will fit grammatically and will even make sense logically, but you must choose the pair that best fits the idea of the sentence.*

*Note that these words are not taken directly from lessons in this book. This exercise is intended to replicate the sentence completion portion of the SAT.*

1. When a company loses one of its most _____ employees, the _____ office must immediately recruit someone to fill the position.
   A. valued, presentable
   B. invaluable, personable
   C. valuable, personnel
   D. inviolable, personalized
   E. evaluated, personal

2. The NASA procurement expert said that we would already have colonies on Mars if only the _____ weren't _____.
   A. cost, prohibitive
   B. atmosphere, poisonous
   C. technology, primitive
   D. distance, great
   E. obstacles, scientific

3. Spending Friday night at the mall became a[n] _____ for many teens in the small town, since it seemed to provide a[n] _____ from their boredom.
   A. ritual, break
   B. occurrence, outlet
   C. problem, escape
   D. challenge, timeout
   E. habit, exchange

4.  Before you retype your entire _____, you should check the
    _____ of the facts in it.
    A.  manuscript, accuracy
    B.  report, number
    C.  book, reliability
    D.  page, quality
    E.  thesis, summary

5.  Math, without any _____, is the subject in which I am _____.
    A.  complaint, capable
    B.  problems, deficient
    C.  competition, weakest
    D.  difficulty, strong
    E.  error, best

6.  The _____ problems of the junk email called *spam*, destructive
    attacks by hackers, and the _____ of computer viruses has prompted
    the near-mandatory use of anti-virus software.
    A.  dual, universality
    B.  concomitant, proliferation
    C.  heinous, profusion
    D.  ludicrous, destruction
    E.  deceitful, fallacies

7.  There's no doubt that the candidate who runs on a platform of _____
    responsibility will get my vote; I believe in _____ the growth of gov-
    ernment spending.
    A.  fiscal, curtailing
    B.  corporate, controlling
    C.  financial, freeing
    D.  individual, limiting
    E.  Congressional, maximizing

8.  During the founder and president's untimely and _____ illness, the
    business endured the worst _____ in its twenty-five-year history.
    A.  ill-planned, catastrophe
    B.  inconceivable, recession
    C.  unfortunate, increase
    D.  lengthy, slowdown
    E.  unnecessary, strike

## EXERCISE II – Crossword Puzzle

*Use the clues to complete the crossword puzzle. The answers consist of vocabulary words from lessons 8 through 14.*

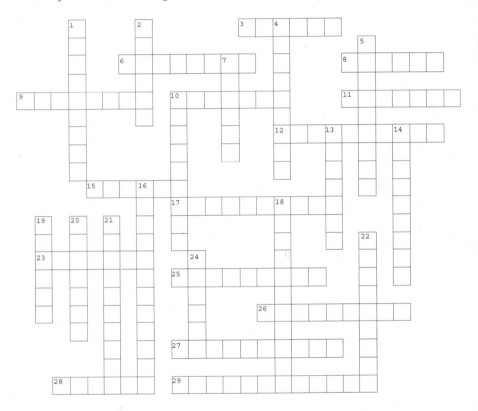

**Across**
3. gaudy
6. healthful
8. to gather
9. rebellion
10. calm
11. rural
12. to expand
15. to frolic
17. weepy
23. sluggish
25. a stopping
26. talkative
27. deceitful
28. warning
29. peculiar trait

**Down**
1. omen
2. to show off
4. repetitious
5. gloomy
7. to draw back
10. the masses
13. clothing
14. domineering
16. flattery
18. evil plan
19. setting
20. to criticize
21. to contaminate
22. hatred
24. to ridicule

# Lesson Fifteen

1. **orifice** (ôr´ ə fis) *n.* mouth; opening
The cavity in his tooth felt like a giant *orifice*, but it actually was quite small.

2. **hallow** (hal´ ō) *v.* to make holy
We cannot *hallow* this field, for the men who died here made it holy.
*syn: bless; consecrate* *ant: desecrate*

3. **perdition** (pər dish´ ən) *n.* damnation; ruin; hell
The sermon was about the sins which lead to *perdition*.

4. **chaff** (chaf) *n.* worthless matter
"Give me just the facts," the professor said. "Separate the wheat from the *chaff.*"
*syn: rubbish*

5. **aesthetic** (es thet´ ik) *adj.* pertaining to beauty
The house was cheap, but it lacked any *aesthetic* qualities.
*syn: artistic* *ant: displeasing; unattractive*

6. **empirical** (em pîr´ i kəl) *adj.* based on practical experience rather than theory
Her theory sounded logical, but the *empirical* data did not support it.
*syn: observable* *ant: theoretical*

7. **germane** (jər mān´) *adj.* relevant; fitting
Make sure that all of your answers are *germane* to the questions.
*syn: appropriate; pertinent; suitable* *ant: irrelevant*

8. **hermetic** (hər met´ ik) *adj.* tightly sealed
That medicine should be packed in *hermetic* containers.
*syn: airtight*

9. **meretricious** (mer i trish´ əs) *adj.* attractive in a cheap, flashy way
She was naturally beautiful, so no one knew why she wore such *meretricious* looking clothing.
*syn: gaudy; showy; tawdry* *ant: restrained; tasteful*

10. **querulous** (kwer´ ə ləs) *adj.* complaining; grumbling
The *querulous* child on the plane annoyed the other passengers.
*syn: fretful; peevish* *ant: complacent; satisfied*

11. **flaccid** (flas´ id) *adj.* flabby
    The retired athlete's muscles became *flaccid* after years without exercise.
    *syn: weak; feeble*                                    *ant: solid; taut*

12. **hospice** (hos´ pis) *n.* a shelter for travelers, orphans, or the ill or
    destitute
    The new *hospice* for cancer patients opened in July.

13. **egregious** (i grē´ jəs) *adj.* remarkably bad; outrageous
    His remark was so *egregious* that it shocked everyone at the party.
    *syn: flagrant; gross*                                *ant: moderate*

14. **ratiocinate** (rash i os´ ə nāt) *v.* to reason; to think
    Because alcohol had dulled his mind, he was no longer able to *ratiocinate*
    clearly.

15. **foment** (fō ment´) *v.* to stir up; to incite
    At the convention, people were hired to *foment* disruptions during the sen-
    ator's speech.
    *syn: instigate; arouse*                              *ant: quell; curb*


## EXERCISE I—Words in Context

*From the list below, supply the words needed to complete the paragraph. Some
words will not be used.*

| aesthetic | orifice | ratiocinate | meretricious |
|-----------|---------|-------------|--------------|
| hospice   | flaccid | chaff       |              |

1.   Low hemlock branches hid the _____ of the cave and kept the rain
     out. The cave didn't compare to the _____ in which Ben had spent
     the previous night, but it was still a better alternative to sleeping in the
     open. As the sun sank behind the wood line, Ben sat on a decaying log and
     _____ about his next move. He was penniless and lost, and while the
     _____ scenery of the old forest was nice to look at, it didn't provide
     the food that Ben would need to survive. The temperature was dropping,
     and his _____, Italian-leather jacket looked sporty but provided little
     warmth.

*From the list below, supply the words needed to complete the paragraph. Some words will not be used.*

| | | | |
|---|---|---|---|
| hallow | perdition | egregious | hospice |
| foment | empirical | querulous | meretricious |

2.  Mrs. Patterson nearly fainted when she read about her son's _____ crime in the police report of the local newspaper. As usual, her _____ son, Tom, blamed everyone else for his crime—his friends, the police, the storeowner, etc. Tom's mother had _____ knowledge about the fate of criminals; Tom's father had regularly _____ authorities, and he died in prison. Mrs. Patterson feared that if Tom didn't _____ himself by abandoning his criminal ways, his life also would end in _____.

*From the list below, supply the words needed to complete the paragraph. Some words will not be used.*

| | | |
|---|---|---|
| germane | chaff | orifice |
| hermetic | flaccid | hallow |

3.  Dedicated to toning her _____ arms and legs, Rita started jogging on three days of the week. Every night, she took a multivitamin from a[n] _____ sealed container. This was absolutely _____ to her fitness goals. She saw too many people rely on pills or protein powders or similar _____ when they really just needed to get up and exercise.

## EXERCISE II—Sentence Completion

*Complete the sentence in a way that shows you understand the meaning of the italicized vocabulary word.*

1.  Max liked to *foment* arguments at the dinner table by…

2.  If you *ratiocinate* too long about how to get to the theater, you will…

3.  People could hear calls for help, but no one wanted to enter the *orifice* of the cave because…

4.  The town *hallowed* the site of the tragic accident; no one was allowed to…

5.  Maggie's parents told her to change her *meretricious* behavior if she wanted to…

6.  The *empirical* data showed the prototype jet would need…

7.  The *hermetic* vials were stored in a safe because they contained…

8.  The *querulous* passenger refused to…

9.  The elderly man was moved to a *hospice* after…

10. Since Dirk thought that he was already headed for *perdition*, he…

11. Terri's *flaccid* excuse for not studying was…

12. Tina could not stand all the *chaff* on television, so she…

13. Johnny's parents grounded him for his *egregious* behavior after he…

14. Include only *germane* information when you take an essay test, or else you will…

15. A state with *aesthetic* mountain scenery will attract tourists because…

## EXERCISE III—Roots, Prefixes, and Suffixes

*Study the entries and answer the questions that follow.*

The root *equ* means "equal."
The roots *flect* and *flex* mean "bend."
The suffix *ity* means "quality of."
The root *nox* means "night."
The suffixes *able* and *ible* mean "able to be."
The prefix *sub* means "secretly."
The root *fug* means "flee."
The prefix *cent* means "center."

1. Using literal translations as guidance, define the following words without using a dictionary.

   A. inflection
   B. flexible
   C. equitable
   D. equinox
   E. subterfuge
   F. centrifuge

2. When you are too cold or too hot, your body will shiver or perspire in order to achieve a state of _____.

3. A suit of armor might _____ the blows of an enemy's sword, but the armor has stiff joints that make the wearer unable to bend, or _____.

4. One who flees from the law is a[n] _____, and one who flees from harm is a[n] _____.

   A *fugue* (or a *round*, such as "Row-Row-Row Your Boat") is a musical composition in which a theme begins in one voice, and is then imitated and built upon by different successive voices at various times throughout the propagation of the melody. Explain the possible reasoning for the word *fugue* having a root that means "to flee."

5. List all the words that you can think of that contain the root *cent*.

## EXERCISE IV—Inference

*Complete the sentences by inferring information about the italicized word from its context.*

1.  Dr. Paxton gathered *empirical* data during the accelerated plant growth experiment by...

2.  Some of the protestors at the World Bank meeting were actually concerned about policies that affect underdeveloped nations, but others went to *foment* trouble by...

3.  The concussion impaired the man's ability to *ratiocinate*, judging by the way in which he...

## EXERCISE V—Writing

*Here is a writing prompt similar to the one you will find on the writing portion of the SAT.*

Plan and write an essay based on the following statement:

> None are so deaf as those who will not hear.
> Of those whose vision's dim where'er they be,
> None are so blind as those who will not see."
> –A Book of Proverbs compiled in 1876

**Assignment:** In an essay, explain the proverb's relevance to the present world. Provide at least one example for each of the proverb's two assertions, that "none are so deaf..." and "none are so blind...." Support your claim using evidence from your reading, studies, personal observations, and experiences.

**Thesis:** Write a one-sentence response to the above assignment. Make certain this single sentence offers a clear statement of your position.

*Example: If true blindness and deafness is an inability to see or hear painful truths, then many modern Americans are both blind and deaf.*

**Organizational Plan:** If your thesis is the point on which you want to end, where does your essay need to begin? List the points of development that are inevitable in leading your reader from your beginning point to your end point. This list is your outline.

**Draft:** Use your thesis as both your beginning and your end. Following your outline, write a good first draft of your essay. Remember to support all your points with examples, facts, references to reading, etc.

**Review and revise:** Exchange essays with a classmate. Using the scoring guide for Sentence Formation and Variety on page 242, score your partner's essay (while he or she scores yours). Focus on the sentence structure and the use of language conventions. If necessary, rewrite your essay to improve the sentence structure and/or your use of language.

## Improving Paragraphs

*Read the following passage and then answer the multiple-choice questions that follow. The questions will require you to make decisions regarding the revision of the reading selection.*

1    Proper care of the teeth and gums is essential for a healthy lifestyle. Ignoring in-depth maintenance of the teeth and surrounding structures can lead to many avoidable problems. Incomplete chewing of food can lead to indigestion and the probability that food is not being properly absorbed, this ultimately results in malnutrition. Teeth function as the nutrition procurement system of the body, and they are also an early warning system of disease. Properly maintaining the mouth is the first step to a lifetime of proper nutrition.

2    As the ultimate in perfectly designed food processors, the mouth handles all nutrients prior to ingestion. Saliva, working in conjunction with teeth, is the first agent to work on the digestion of food. The normal pH of saliva is slightly acidic, but it can be neutralized with an alkaline mouthwash such as baking soda and water. Cleaning the teeth after meals also helps to maintain the proper pH level of the mouth.

3    As procurement officers, teeth are designed to grab, tear and grind fueling substances that empower the body to do work. For the teeth to be effective as blenders providing fortification for the body, they need to be properly aligned. The grinding teeth the upper and lower molars fit face to face on every plane so that when they come together they are in exact alignment to mash food into digestible form. If nature has not seen to their precise alignment, an orthodontist may be called in to make suitable adjustments. Designer braces are available for those who can afford them. Thanks to dental technology, braces and retainers are no longer an inconvenient or unsightly way to ensure proper alignment.

4      Proper care of the teeth includes brushing up and down to remove tiny food particles and bacteria. Flossing can be helpful when teeth are so close together that a brush cannot clear the spaces in-between. If thorough maintenance is applied to the teeth every day, they should never need replacement. Dentures are considered a replacement but never do the job as well.

1. Which of the following changes best corrects an error in paragraph 1?
   A. Hyphenate *nutrition procurement system.*
   B. Capitalize *disease.*
   C. Combine the first two sentences.
   D. Change *essential for* to *essential to.*
   E. Place a semicolon after *absorbed.*

2. Which sentence in paragraph 1 should be moved to paragraph 3?
   A. sentence 1
   B. sentence 2
   C. sentence 3
   D. sentence 4
   E. sentence 5

3. If you had to delete a sentence in paragraph 3, which would be the most appropriate choice?
   A. sentence 1
   B. sentence 2
   C. sentence 3
   D. sentence 4
   E. sentence 5

4. Which of the following suggestions would correct an omission in the third paragraph?
   A. Add hyphens to *face to face.*
   B. Capitalize *orthodontist.*
   C. Insert commas around the appositive, "the upper and lower molars."
   D. Set off "the upper and lower molars" with dashes.
   E. Change *nature* to read *Mother Nature.*

5. Which of the following suggestions would improve the concluding paragraph?
   A. Delete the last sentence.
   B. Move sentence 4 to precede sentence 1.
   C. Reverse the order of all the sentences.
   D. Exchange sentences 2 and 4.
   E. Eliminate the paragraph.

# Lesson Sixteen

1. **salient** (sā´ lē ənt) *adj.* significant; conspicuous; standing out from the rest
   The judge advised the attorney to stick to the *salient* facts of the case.
   *syn: important*

2. **recant** (ri kant´) *v.* to withdraw or disavow a statement or opinion
   The suspect *recanted* his confession, so the police had to release him.

3. **jocular** (jok´ yə lər) *adj.* humorous; lighthearted
   Dad's *jocular* manner faded when he started preparing the taxes.
   *syn: joking; witty; amusing*          *ant: solemn; morose*

4. **palliate** (pal´ ē āt) *v.* to ease; to lessen; to soothe
   She became a nurse to *palliate* suffering, but all she had done so far was record temperatures.
   *syn: alleviate; excuse*          *ant: intensify; exacerbate*

5. **malleable** (mal´ ē ə bəl) *adj.* capable of being changed; easily shaped
   The sculptor wanted to keep the clay *malleable* until he was sure of the final design.
   *syn: workable*          *ant: rigid; inflexible*

6. **recreant** (rek´ rē ənt) *n.* a coward; a traitor
   Benedict Arnold is one of the most famous *recreants* in history.

7. **affinity** (ə fin´ i tē) *n.* an attraction to
   The young man had an *affinity* for fast cars and easy money.
   *syn: partiality; fondness*          *ant: aversion*

8. **impalpable** (im pāl´ pə bəl) *adj.* unable to be felt; intangible
   He was aware of some *impalpable* fear as he entered the room.
   *syn: imperceptible; indiscernible*

9. **fiscal** (fis´ kəl) *adj.* pertaining to finances
   December is the accountant's busiest month because it is the end of the *fiscal* year.
   *syn: economic; budgetary*

10. **regale** (ri gāl´) *v.* to delight with something pleasing or amusing
    John *regaled* the crowd for hours with his stories of Scotland.
    *syn: entertain; amuse*          *ant: anger; depress; annoy*

11. **miscreant**   (mis´ krē ənt)   *n.*   a vicious person
    The police were looking for the *miscreant* in all of the local hangouts.
    *syn: villain; criminal; knave*

12. **flagellate**   (flaj´ ə lāt)   *v.*   to whip; to lash
    The boy's father never struck him, but he *flagellated* him verbally.
    *syn: flog*

13. **lascivious**   (la siv´ ē əs)   *adj.*   lustful or lewd
    His *lascivious* smile disgusted the other people in the room.
    *syn: wanton; obscene*                         *ant: wholesome; decent*

14. **flout**   (flout)   *v.*   to ridicule; to show contempt for
    He broke the rules and *flouted* all authority, and now he has to pay.
    *syn: mock; scoff*                              *ant: esteem; revere*

15. **salacious**   (sə lā´ shəs)   *adj.*   obscene; lustful
    The minister denounced the movie because of its *salacious* nature.
    *syn: lecherous*                                *ant: chaste*

## EXERCISE I—Words in Context

*From the list below, supply the words needed to complete the paragraph. Some words will not be used.*

| | | | |
|---|---|---|---|
| **salient** | **miscreant** | **flout** | **affinity** |
| **recant** | **salacious** | **jocular** | |

1.   The actor was a[n] _____ who regularly _____ the law. Tabloid reporters followed him around all day, hoping to catch his _____ behavior on film. He had a[n] _____ for dive bars in bad neighborhoods. The reporters paid for any _____, negative information on him.

*From the list below, supply the words needed to complete the paragraph. Some words will not be used.*

| | | |
|---|---|---|
| **palliate** | **flout** | **flagellate** |
| **fiscal** | **recant** | **lascivious** |

2.   The Puritan leaders of Salem decided to _____ Sara for the _____ crime of dancing on the Sabbath. Sara was lucky that the judge had _____ her punishment; her friend, Abigail, was sentenced to death because she refused to _____ a statement about the town's religious practices.

*From the list below, supply the words needed to complete the paragraph. Some words will not be used.*

| | | | |
|---|---|---|---|
| **jocular** | **fiscal** | **affinity** | **recreant** |
| **malleable** | **impalpable** | **regale** | **flagellate** |

3.   The two _____ who had run away from the battle were engaged in _____ conversation when the search team surprised them. The cowards had stolen the battalion's treasury and _____ themselves with the thought of securing their _____ futures. They had planned to melt the _____ gold coins into bars and sell them on the black market. The weight of leg irons, however, helped them to snap out of their _____ dream.

## EXERCISE II—Sentence Completion

*Complete the sentence in a way that shows you understand the meaning of the italicized vocabulary word.*

1. The senator *recanted* his controversial statement, because it...

2. The surgeon *palliated* the patient's fears by...

3. The *recreant* was temporarily happy to have escaped the fighting, but when the other soldiers found him, he...

4. Greg did not understand the *impalpable,* sad meaning of the poem...

5. Helen *regaled* the family by telling them about...

6. The buggy driver *flagellated* the horses in an attempt to...

7. Rachel *flouted* the rules at the rock concert, so the guards...

8. The engine and wheels are *salient* parts of...

9. It is good to see Jason is such a *jocular* mood for a change; he is usually...

10. Teenagers with *malleable* beliefs are susceptible to cults because...

11. Caleb has an *affinity* for Cajun food, but Allison prefers to...

12. Stormtech, a huge corporation, uses its vast *fiscal* powers to...

13. When the police cornered the *miscreant* in the alley, he...

14. Some networks refuse to broadcast *lascivious* programs because...

15. Brandon brought a *salacious* magazine to class, so the teacher...

## EXERCISE III—Roots, Prefixes, and Suffixes

*Study the entries and answer the questions that follow.*

The root *derm* means "skin."
The root *fer* means "to bear" or "to carry."
The prefix *in* means "into" or "against."
The prefix *suf*, *sub*, and *sus* mean "under" or "secretly."
The prefix *epi* means "upon," "over," or "above."
The prefix *de* means "down" or "off."
The suffix *al* means "pertaining to."
The suffix *itis* means "inflammation of."

1. Using literal translations as guidance, define the following words without using a dictionary.

   A. tendinitis      D. fertile
   B. suffer      E. infer
   C. epicenter      F. subdermal

2. An inflammation of the skin is a form of _____, and the best doctor to treat it is a[n] _____.

3. Literally, *transfer* means _____ _____.

   If a reading passage carries a thought to an outside idea, then the passage _____ to that idea.

   If you need to put off a payment until next month, you might ask the bank to _____ the payment until you have money.

4. List as many words as you can think of that contain the root *fer*.

5. List as many words as you can think of that end with the suffix *al*.

## EXERCISE IV—Inference

*Complete the sentences by inferring information about the italicized word from its context.*

1. The *recreant* received icy stares from his fellow soldiers because he had…

2. The arthritic artist preferred sculpting *malleable* clay to chiseling hard granite because the clay is…

3. Brook did not like crowds, but she had such an *affinity* for the band that she took herself to…

## EXERCISE V—Critical Reading

*Below is a pair of reading passages followed by several multiple-choice questions similar to the ones you will encounter on the SAT. Carefully read both passages and choose the best answer to each of the questions.*

*The first passage is an excerpt from the final chapter of Leo Tolstoy's novella, <u>The Death of Ivan Ilyich</u> (1886). In this passage, Ivan, an uninteresting bureaucrat on his deathbed, comes to terms with the spiritless life that he lived.*

*The second passage is an excerpt from a chapter of <u>Sketches by Boz</u>, a collection of stories by Charles Dickens, first published in 1836. Chapter Twelve, "A Visit to Newgate," is Dickens's creative account of a visit to Victorian London's dreadful Newgate Prison. In this excerpt from the chapter, Dickens observes a condemned prisoner awaiting execution.*

**Passage 1**

For three whole days, during which time did not exist for him, he struggled in that black sack into which he was being thrust by an invisible, resistless force. He struggled as a man condemned to death struggles in the hands of the executioner, knowing that he cannot save himself. And every moment he felt that despite all his
5   efforts he was drawing nearer and nearer to what terrified him. He felt that his agony was due to his being thrust into that black hole and still more to his not being able to get right into it. He was hindered from getting into it by his conviction that his life had been a good one. That very justification of his life held him fast and prevented his moving forward, and it caused him most torment of all.
10   Suddenly some force struck him in the chest and side, making it still harder to breathe, and he fell through the hole and there at the bottom was a light. What had

happened to him was like the sensation one sometimes experiences in a railway carriage when one thinks one is going backwards while one is really going forwards and suddenly becomes aware of the real direction.

15    "Yes, it was not the right thing," he said to himself, "but that's no matter. It can be done. But what *is* the right thing?" he asked himself, and suddenly grew quiet.

This occurred at the end of the third day, two hours before his death. Just then his schoolboy son had crept softly in and gone up to the bedside. The dying man was still screaming desperately and waving his arms. His hand fell on the boy's
20    head, and the boy caught it, pressed it to his lips, and began to cry.

At that very moment Ivan Ilych fell through and caught sight of the light, and it was revealed to him that though his life had not been what it should have been, this could still be rectified. He asked himself, "What is the right thing?" and grew still, listening. Then he felt that someone was kissing his hand. He opened his eyes,
25    looked at his son, and felt sorry for him. His wife came up to him and he glanced at her. She was gazing at him open-mouthed, with undried tears on her nose and cheek and a despairing look on her face. He felt sorry for her too.

"Yes, I am making them wretched," he thought. "They are sorry, but it will be better for them when I die." He wished to say this but had not the strength to utter it.
30    "Besides, why speak? I must act," he thought. With a look at his wife he indicated his son and said: "Take him away...sorry for him...sorry for you too...." He tried to add, "Forgive me," but said "Forego" and waved his hand, knowing that He whose understanding mattered would understand.

35    And suddenly it grew clear to him that what had been oppressing him and would not leave his was all dropping away at once from two sides, from ten sides, and from all sides. He was sorry for them, he must act so as not to hurt them: release them and free himself from these sufferings. "How good and how simple!" he thought. "And the pain?" he asked himself. "What has become of it? Where are you, pain?"
40    He turned his attention to it.

"Yes, here it is. Well, what of it? Let the pain be."

"And death...where is it?"

He sought his former accustomed fear of death and did not find it. "Where is it? What death?" There was no fear because there was no death.
45    In place of death there was light.

"So that's what it is!" he suddenly exclaimed aloud. "What joy!"

To him all this happened in a single instant, and the meaning of that instant did not change. For those present his agony continued for another two hours. Something rattled in his throat, his emaciated body twitched, then the gasping and
50    rattle became less and less frequent.

"It is finished!" said someone near him.

He heard these words and repeated them in his soul.

"Death is finished," he said to himself. "It is no more!"

He drew in a breath, stopped in the midst of a sigh, stretched out, and died.

**Passage 2**

We entered the first cell. It was a stone dungeon, eight feet long by six wide, with a bench at the upper end, under which were a common rug, a bible, and prayer-book. An iron candlestick was fixed into the wall at the side; and a small high window in the back admitted as much air and light as could struggle in between a
5 double row of heavy, crossed iron bars. It contained no other furniture of any description.

Conceive the situation of a man, spending his last night on earth in this cell. Buoyed up with some vague and undefined hope of reprieve, he knew not why—indulging in some wild and visionary idea of escaping, he knew not how—hour
10 after hour of the three preceding days allowed him for preparation, has fled with a speed which no man living would deem possible, for none but this dying man can know. He has wearied his friends with entreaties, exhausted the attendants with importunities, neglected in his feverish restlessness the timely warnings of his spiritual consoler; and, now that the illusion is at last dispelled, now that eternity is
15 before him and guilt behind, now that his fears of death amount almost to madness, and an overwhelming sense of his helpless, hopeless state rushes upon him, he is lost and stupefied, and has neither thoughts to turn to, nor power to call upon, the Almighty Being, from whom alone he can seek mercy and forgiveness, and before whom his repentance can alone avail.

20 Hours have glided by, and still he sits upon the same stone bench with folded arms, heedless alike of the fast decreasing time before him, and the urgent entreaties of the good man at his side. The feeble light is wasting gradually, and the deathlike stillness of the street without, broken only by the rumbling of some passing vehicle which echoes mournfully through the empty yards, warns him that the
25 night is waning fast away. The deep bell of St. Paul's strikes—one! He heard it; it has roused him. Seven hours left! He paces the narrow limits of his cell with rapid strides, cold drops of terror starting on his forehead, and every muscle of his frame quivering with agony. Seven hours! He suffers himself to be led to his seat, mechanically takes the bible which is placed in his hand, and tries to read and listen. No:
30 his thoughts will wander. The book is torn and soiled by use—and like the book he read his lessons in, at school, just forty years ago! He has never bestowed a thought upon it, perhaps, since he left it as a child: and yet the place, the time, the room—nay, the very boys he played with, crowd as vividly before him as if they were scenes of yesterday; and some forgotten phrase, some childish word, rings in his ears like
35 the echo of one uttered but a minute since. The voice of the clergyman recalls him to himself. He is reading from the sacred book its solemn promises of pardon for repentance, and its awful denunciation of obdurate men. He falls upon his knees and clasps his hands to pray. Hush! what sound was that? He starts upon his feet. It cannot be two yet. Hark! Two quarters have struck;—the third—the fourth. It is!
40 Six hours left! Tell him not of repentance! Six hours' repentance for eight times six years of guilt and sin! He buries his face in his hands, and throws himself on the bench.

Worn with watching and excitement, he sleeps, and the same unsettled state of mind pursues him in his dreams. An insupportable load is taken from his breast; he
45 is walking with his wife in a pleasant field, with the bright sky above them, and a fresh and boundless prospect on every side—how different from the stone walls of

Newgate! She is looking—not as she did when he saw her for the last time in that dreadful place, but as she used when he loved her—long, long ago, before misery and ill-treatment had altered her looks, and vice had changed his nature, and she is
50 leaning upon his arm, and looking up into his face with tenderness and affection—and he does NOT strike her now, nor rudely shake her from him. And oh! how glad he is to tell her all he had forgotten in that last hurried interview, and to fall on his knees before her and fervently beseech her pardon for all the unkindness and cruelty that wasted her form and broke her heart! The scene suddenly changes. He is
55 on his trial again: there are the judge and jury, and prosecutors, and witnesses, just as they were before. How full the court is—what a sea of heads—with a gallows, too, and a scaffold—and how all those people stare at HIM! Verdict, 'Guilty.' No matter; he will escape.

The night is dark and cold, the gates have been left open, and in an instant he is
60 in the street, flying from the scene of his imprisonment like the wind. The streets are cleared, the open fields are gained and the broad, wide country lies before him. Onward he dashes in the midst of darkness, over hedge and ditch, through mud and pool, bounding from spot to spot with a speed and lightness, astonishing even to himself. At length he pauses; he must be safe from pursuit now; he will stretch
65 himself on that bank and sleep till sunrise.

A period of unconsciousness succeeds. He wakes, cold and wretched. The dull, gray light of morning is stealing into the cell, and falls upon the form of the attendant turnkey. Confused by his dreams, he starts from his uneasy bed in momentary uncertainty. It is but momentary. Every object in the narrow cell is too frightfully
70 real to admit of doubt or mistake. He is the condemned felon again, guilty and despairing; and in two hours more will be dead.

1.  In paragraph 1 of the first passage, "being thrust into that black hole" is a metaphor for
    A. repentance.
    B. the inability to remember.
    C. falling asleep.
    D. dying.
    E. justifying one's life.

2.  Which of the following best paraphrases this sentence from lines 31–33 of the first passage?

    > He tried to add, "Forgive me," but said "Forego" and waved his hand, knowing that He whose understanding mattered would understand.

    A. It didn't matter if his family understood him, because God would not understand.
    B. Ivan never really cared for his family, so it did not matter if they failed to understand him.
    C. He knew that God understood him, and that, unlike his family understanding him, mattered.
    D. He knew that God understood him, which mattered more than his family understanding him.
    E. What Ivan understood did not matter, unlike what his family understood.

3.  The first passage is best described as
    A. a satire of the last few hours of Ivan Ilych's life.
    B. an autobiographical sketch of Ivan Ilych.
    C. an account of Ivan Ilyich's perception of his impending death.
    D. Leo Tolstoy's attempt to depict himself in fiction.
    E. a response to Charles Dickens's *Sketches by Boz*.

4.  What has *fled* in paragraph 2 of the second passage?
    A. the prisoner's imagination
    B. the will to seek redemption
    C. the prisoner's hopes of escape
    D. the fears of death
    E. the hours preceding the execution

5. According to paragraph 3 of the second passage, the prisoner is
   A. 28 years old.
   B. 33 years old.
   C. 40 years old.
   D. 48 years old.
   E. 56 years old.

6. Which of the following best states the implication of this line from passage 2 (lines 49–51)?

   > …she is leaning upon his arm, and looking up into his face with tenderness and affection—and he does NOT strike her now, nor rudely shake her from him.

   A. The prisoner does not understand why he cannot strike his wife.
   B. The prisoner used to physically abuse his wife.
   C. The prisoner and his wife do not usually get along.
   D. The prisoner has a terrible temper.
   E. The prisoner and his wife have not seen each other for years.

7. As used in line 67 of the second passage, *stealing* most nearly means
   A. taking without permission.
   B. leaving.
   C. forging.
   D. creating a metallic shine.
   E. creeping.

8. One emotion that the central characters of both passages feel is
   A. remorse for hurting their families.
   B. awe for the unknown.
   C. remorse for their own situations.
   D. arrogance toward death.
   E. fear of not repenting.

9. Which of the following best describes the difference in situation between the main characters in each of the passages?
   A. Ivan handles death much better than the prisoner does.
   B. The prisoner does not exhibit any regret, while Ivan apologizes.
   C. Ivan is physically dying, while the prisoner is waiting to be killed.
   D. Ivan dies, but the prisoner escapes death.
   E. The prisoner is already dead, but Ivan is about to die.

10. Which of the following is a subject shared by both passages?
    A. accepting fate
    B. mistreatment of prisoners
    C. family communication
    D. the benefits of optimism
    E. writing narratives

# Lesson Seventeen

1.  **rebuke**  (ri byōōk´)  *v.*  to scold; to blame
    The professor *rebuked* his students for not studying for the exam.
    *syn: admonish; reprimand*          *ant: praise; laud*

2.  **nonentity**  (non en´ ti tē)  *n.*  a person or thing of little importance
    "I'm right here!" she yelled, "but you treat me as a *nonentity*."
    *syn: cipher; nobody*

3.  **sang-froid**  (sän frwa´)  *n.*  calmness; composure or cool self-possession
    The speaker maintained his *sang-froid* despite the heckler's comments.
    *syn: aplomb; self-confidence*          *ant: uneasiness; perturbation*

4.  **desultory**  (des´ əl tôr ē)  *adj.*  wandering from subject to subject
    He gave his talk in such a *desultory* fashion it was hard to understand.
    *syn: disconnected; rambling*

5.  **hector**  (hek´ tər)  *v.*  to bully; to pester
    If you don't take a stand, that bully will *hector* you for the rest of the year.
    *syn: badger; browbeat*

6.  **pandemic**  (pan dem´ ik)  *adj.*  general; widespread
    The Center for Disease Control announced that the disease has become *pandemic*.

7.  **coalesce**  (kō ə les´)  *v.*  to blend; to merge
    The citizens overcame their differences and *coalesced* to rebuild the town after the hurricane.
    *syn: mix; unite; combine*          *ant: separate; divide*

8.  **beguile**  (bi gīl´)  *v.*  to deceive; to charm; to enchant
    Scarlet O'Hara tried to *beguile* all the eligible men she met.
    *syn: charm; fool*          *ant: irritate; bore*

9.  **ennui**  (än wē´)  *n.*  boredom; a weariness resulting from a lack of interest
    The speaker sensed the *ennui* of the audience,  so he told a joke.
                              *ant: excitement; interest*

10. **hiatus**  (hī ā´ təs)  *n.*  a pause or gap
    If you take a *hiatus* in your studies, you might forget the things you have learned.
    *syn: intermission; break*

11. **lambent** (lam´ bənt) *adj.* softly bright or radiant; moving lightly over a
surface
The *lambent* flames cast shadows throughout the cabin.
*syn: glowing; lucid*

12. **ergo** (ûr´ gō) *conj.* therefore
I am broke; *ergo*, I can't pay the rent this week.
*syn: consequently; hence*

13. **hubris** (hyōō´ bris) *n.* excessive pride or self-confidence
The Greek warriors were known for their *hubris* and their fierceness in
battle.
*syn: arrogance; overconfidence*　　　　　　　*ant: humility; diffidence*

14. **pecuniary** (pi kyōō´ nē er´ ē) *adj.* pertaining to money; financial
Jill faced many *pecuniary* troubles after losing her job.
*syn: monetary*

15. **sibilant** (sib´ ə lənt) *adj.* a hissing sound
The guide stopped moving when he heard the *sibilant* sound of a snake.

## EXERCISE I—Words in Context

*From the list below, supply the words needed to complete the paragraph. Some words will not be used.*

| | | | |
|---|---|---|---|
| **ennui** | **hiatus** | **ergo** | **pandemic** |
| **sang-froid** | **hubris** | **rebuke** | **sibilant** |

1. Bill, a hazardous-materials cleanup technician, kept his _____ when he heard the _____ sound of air escaping from his breathing apparatus. His air was running out, but he had to close the valve on the chemical tank before _____ contamination forced the city to evacuate. As he struggled to turn the valve, Bill _____ himself for not inspecting his equipment more often. Six months earlier, an injury had forced Bill to take a[n] _____ from his career, and the _____ of doing nothing had been more painful to him than the chemical burn. He had returned to duty with renewed _____, but now feared it might get him killed.

*From the list below, supply the words needed to complete the paragraph. Some words will not be used.*

| | | | |
|---|---|---|---|
| **nonentity** | **pecuniary** | **ergo** | **beguile** |
| **hector** | **ennui** | **lambent** | **desultory** |
| **hiatus** | **coalesce** | | |

2. Anne's _____ worries made it hard for her to concentrate on her roommate's _____ rambling. Bill collectors _____ Anne every day, and she knew that her next check would not stop them. She gazed at the _____ patterns of light that the aquarium cast on the floor, while allowing moneymaking ideas to _____ in her head. Anne had already tried to _____ her boss into letting her work more hours, but the company regarded college students as _____ who did not warrant full-time jobs. She needed to make enough money to pay for the next semester; _____, Anne would have to find a better job.

## EXERCISE II—Sentence Completion

*Complete the sentence in a way that shows you understand the meaning of the italicized vocabulary word.*

1. When the bank saw that Cole had had *pecuniary* troubles in the past, it refused to…

2. I will not go out to dinner with you; *ergo*,…

3. Adam wanted to teach again, but the *hiatus* in his career was so long that…

4. The vacuum cleaner salesman *beguiled* the couple into believing…

5. Jazz was conceived in the United States, but its *pandemic* growth…

6. The suspect's *desultory* alibi convinced the police that…

7. While discussing colleges, Alexa's parents said that her boyfriend is a *nonentity* and that he should not influence…

8. Lucas *rebuked* the dog for…

9. A fireman who loses his *sang-froid* while fighting a fire may…

10. During the company strike, some of the picketers *hectored* the people who continued…

11. The auto-body repair shop *coalesced* all its records so that…

12. To Leslie, the board meeting was two hours of *ennui*, and it would be difficult for her to…

13. The *lambent* moonlight reflected on the surface of…

14. The general's *hubris* frightened the soldiers, because they were not sure that they could…

15. When Courtney heard the *sibilant* noise coming from the tire, she knew that…

## EXERCISE III—Roots, Prefixes, and Suffixes

*Study the entries and answer the questions that follow.*

The root *lud* means "to play" or "to mock."
The root *grav* means "heavy."
The root *son* means "sound" or "to sound."
The root *und* means "wave," "to surge," or "to flood."
The prefix *ab* means "to flow."
The prefix *inter* means "between" or "among."

1.  Using literal translations as guidance, define the following words without using a dictionary.

    A.  elude                      D.  sonic
    B.  ludicrous                  E.  gravity
    C.  illusion                   F.  undulate

2.  The _____ to the play consisted of a narrator describing the setting before the curtain opened. An orchestra played musical _____ between acts while the theater crew rearranged the stage.

3.  A[n] _____ situation has heavy consequences, and if you _____ the problem, then you will add to it.

4.  The alphabet consists of sounds that we call vowels and _____.
    If the members of a chorus all sing together, then they are said to be singing in _____.

    William Shakespeare is famous for his drama and his _____, or poems consisting of fourteen lines.

5.  A[n] _____ essay is flooded with extra words, and its unnecessary length might _____ readers.

## EXERCISE IV—Inference

*Complete the sentences by inferring information about the italicized word from its context.*

1.  The cockroach is a *pandemic* insect; most of the people on Earth would probably be able to...


2.  Joshua's *hubris* cost him a scholarship because he spent the evening watching television instead of preparing for...


3.  Tim thought that his thoughts were too *desultory* for him to become a pharmacist; he worried that he might fill the wrong prescription because he...

# EXERCISE V—Writing

Here is a writing prompt similar to the one you will find on the writing portion of the SAT.

Plan and write an essay based on the following statement:

> Author Anna Quindlen wrote in *How Reading Changed My Life,* "I did not read from a sense of superiority, or advancement, or even learning. I read because I loved it more than any other activity on earth."
>
> One activity that is as important to me as reading was to Anna Quindlen is…

**Assignment:** Write an essay in which you discuss the importance of the activity that you have noted above. Support any generalities with specific references to the activity you are discussing and to your experience and observations.

**Thesis:** Write a one-sentence response to the above assignment. Make certain this single sentence offers a clear statement of your position.

*Example: For me, bicycling is more than a pleasant way to spend a Saturday afternoon; it is how I cleanse my mind and spirit and remind myself to aspire to greatness in the things that I do.*

**Organizational Plan:** If your thesis is the point on which you want to end, where does your essay need to begin? List the points of development that are inevitable in leading your reader from your beginning point to your end point. This list is your outline.

**Draft:** Use your thesis as both your beginning and your end. Following your outline, write a good first draft of your essay. Remember to support all your points with examples, facts, references to reading, etc.

**Review and revise:** Exchange essays with a classmate. Using the scoring guide for Word Choice on page 243, score your partner's essay (while he or she scores yours). Focus on word choice and the use of language conventions. If necessary, rewrite your essay to improve your word choice and/or your use of language.

## Identifying Sentence Errors

*Identify the grammatical error in each of the following sentences. If the sentence contains no error, select answer choice E.*

1.  By the time Joe <u>finally</u> got <u>a job he</u> had applied to <u>more than</u> fifty
                    (A)              (B)                        (C)
    <u>companies</u>.   <u>No error</u>
    (D)              (E)

2.  Has the coach <u>chose</u> the <u>new uniforms</u> for the <u>soccer team</u>  <u>yet?</u>  <u>No error</u>
                   (A)           (B)                  (C)          (D)       (E)

3.  <u>Anyone</u> seeking articles <u>lost at the theater</u>  <u>may check</u> lost and found
       (A)                         (B)                    (C)
    <u>for their items</u>.    <u>No error</u>
       (D)                (E)

4.  Dave <u>is so ill</u> that he <u>has done</u> nothing <u>but lay</u> on the bed <u>all day</u>.
            (A)                 (B)                (C)                   (D)
    <u>No error</u>
       (E)

5.  Young <u>people,</u>  <u>like you and I</u>, have so many career options
             (A)          (B)
    <u>available that it</u> is <u>hard to</u> make a selection.      <u>No error</u>
       (C)                     (D)                            (E)

## Improving Sentences

*The underlined portion of each sentence below contains some flaw. Select the answer choice that best corrects the flaw.*

6. The thief ran up behind her, <u>grabs the woman's purse,</u> and ran around a corner before anyone could see his face.
   A. grabbed the woman's purse
   B. grabs the women's purse
   C. grabbed the womens purses
   D. grabs the purse of the woman
   E. the woman's purse was taken

7. Jane has excellent qualifications not only as a scientist <u>but she knows a lot about management, too.</u>
   A. and she likes science, too.
   B. but also in the skills of management.
   C. but also as a manager.
   D. but in the knowledge of management.
   E. but also managing.

8. Lucy baked <u>chocolate chip cookies to give her friends with walnuts.</u>
   A. walnuts with chocolate chip cookies to give her friends.
   B. chocolate chip cookies with walnuts.
   C. chocolate chip cookies for her friends to give.
   D. to give her friends, chocolate chip cookies with walnuts.
   E. chocolate chip cookies with walnuts to give her friends.

9. Our boss called <u>a meeting in relation to</u> the sales project.
   A. a meeting about
   B. a discussion session in relation to
   C. to tell us to meet to talk about
   D. to chit chat about
   E. about

10. Monk Pond is <u>much more shallower than</u> Goodman's Lake.
    A. lesser in depth then
    B. much less deeper than
    C. not nearly so deep as
    D. much more shallow than
    E. much less deep than

# Lesson Eighteen

1. **incendiary**  (in sen´ dē er ē)  *adj.*  causing to excite or inflame
The speaker was not invited back because his *incendiary* behavior caused a riot.
*syn: instigative; inciting*

2. **apotheosis**  (ə pä thē ō´səs)  *n.*  the finest example
The British Parliament has become the *apotheosis* of parliamentary government and serves as a model for many other nations around the world.
*syn: epitome; archetype*

3. **contiguous**  (kən tig´ ū wəs)  *adj.*  making contact or touching at some point; side by side
New Jersey and New York are *contiguous* states because they share a common boundary.
*syn: adjoining; abutting*                    *ant: separated; detached*

4. **auspicious**  (o spi´ shəs)  *adj.*  signaling favorable or promising results
The dark clouds were an *auspicious* sign that rain would fall on the withered fields.
*syn: encouraging*

5. **vociferous**  (vō si´ fə rəs)  *adj.*  marked by noise; loud
The *vociferous*  yelling of the crowd seemed to inspire the team toward victory.
*syn: boisterous; clamorous*

6. **avuncular**  (ə vung´ kyə lər)  *adj.*  similar to an uncle
Martin was not related to the children, but he had an *avuncular* role in raising them.

7. **proletariat**  (prō lə ter´ ē ət)  *n.*  working class or lower class
While many of the rich lived in the hills surrounding the town, the *proletariat* lived in the valley near where they worked.

8. **tenacious**  (tə nā´ shəs)  *adj.*  strongly held; not easy to separate
No one could break the child's *tenacious* grip on the doll.
*syn: clinging; resolute*                    *ant: weak*

9. **specious**  (spē´ shəs)  *adj.*  deceptive or misleading
The *specious* advertisement depicts the run-down resort as a heavenly place.
*syn: false*                    *ant: accurate*

10. **refractory** (ri frak´ tə rē) *adj.* unmanageable or difficult to control; willful
The *refractory* group of boys refused to stop joking with each other during class.
*syn: defiant; provocative*　　　　　　　　*ant: obedient; conforming*

11. **inimitable** (i ni´ mə tə bəl) *adj.* cannot be imitated
The actress was famous for her *inimitable* techniques.
*syn: incomparable; unparalleled*

12. **malfeasance** (mal fēz´ əns) *n.* poor conduct or wrongdoing, especially on the part of a public official
The *malfeasance* of the congressman caused an investigation into his personal conduct.
*syn: corruption; crookedness*

13. **platonic** (plə tä´ nik) *adj.* marked by the absence of romance or physical attraction
Gayle and Robert's *platonic* friendship was based on similar interests and not on romantic interest.

14. **pontificate** (pän ti´ fə kāt) *v.* speak in a pretentiously dignified or dogmatic way
The prosecutor *pontificated* about the defendant's considerable criminal record.
*syn: orate; sermonize*

15. **prurient** (prur´ ē ənt) *adj.* given to lustful or lewd thoughts
Sean's weak willpower often led him to *prurient* activities that were of a questionable nature.
*syn: obscene*

## EXERCISE I—Words in Context

*From the list below, supply the words needed to complete the paragraph. Some words will not be used.*

| | | | |
|---|---|---|---|
| tenacious | inimitable | auspicious | platonic |
| vociferous | pontificate | proletariat | |

1.  The economist, famous for his _____ style of speaking, claimed the shrinking _____ and growing middle class was a[n]_____ sign that the nation's economy was maturing properly. In addition, despite _____ cries to the contrary, he insisted that the nation would need to break its _____ dependence on fossil fuels and develop new forms of technology.

*From the list below, supply the words needed to complete the paragraph. Some words will not be used.*

| | | | |
|---|---|---|---|
| refractory | malfeasance | avuncular | specious |
| contiguous | platonic | vociferous | |

2.  Ed and Diane have a[n] _____ friendship, though many often mistake them for husband and wife. Ed, whose front lawn is _____ with Diane's lawn, is a[n] _____ friend to Diane's children. He cares for them as a father would, though their _____, innocent faces belie their _____ tendencies.

*From the list below, supply the words needed to complete the paragraph. Some words will not be used.*

| | | | |
|---|---|---|---|
| pontificate | malfeasance | contiguous | apotheosis |
| incendiary | proletariat | prurient | |

3.  Thousands of citizens phoned the network with _____ remarks about the _____ halftime show that featured scantily-clad dancers. Some considered the show to be a[n] _____ of the head of the network, and others described the show as the _____ of a declining culture. Talk show hosts and political speakers _____ about the display for weeks after the game.

## EXERCISE II— Sentence Completion

*Complete the sentence in a way that shows you understand the meaning of the italicized vocabulary word.*

1.  Ethan could no longer stand his neighbor's *vociferous* parties, so he…

2.  On the tour of the castle, the guide *pontificated* about…

3.  Your sculpture is not exactly the *apotheosis* of fine art, so stop complaining about the way I…

4.  Matthews is an *avuncular* friend to the children; sometimes he takes them…

5.  Ashley has only *platonic* relationships with coworkers because she believes that…

6.  Texas is the largest of the *contiguous* forty-eight…

7.  When the owners of the steel mills refused to raise wages, the *proletariat*…

8.  When people in the town complained about the teacher's *prurient* night life, the administration decided to…

9.  Allison did not bother to curb her *incendiary* remarks in her letter to…

10. The *auspicious* blossoms on the orange trees gave the farmers hope that the frost had not…

11. Julia kept a *tenacious* grip on her purse whenever she…

12. The governor denied any *malfeasance* on her behalf, but the investigating committee…

13. The husband and wife spy team made *specious* comments about their life; he said that he held a job as…

14. The artist's *inimitable* style makes her work impossible to…

15. Nicole hated walking the *refractory* group of dogs down the street because they…

## EXERCISE III—Roots, Prefixes, and Suffixes

*Study the entries and answer the questions that follow.*

The root *mut* means "to change."
The root *oper* means "to work."
The root *pet* means "to seek" or "to go toward."
The prefix *in* means "against" or "not."
The prefix *per* means "through" or "completely."
The prefix *com* means "together."

1. Using literal translations as guidance, define the following words without using a dictionary.

   A. petition          D. perpetual
   B. impetus           E. cooperate
   C. transmute         F. operation

2. A change to something is a[n] _____, and things that cannot be changed are said to be _____.

   Members of a parole board might meet together and decide to change, or _____, an inmate's prison sentence.

3. Opposing teams _____ by going, or working, toward a goal, and this act of going toward something together is called a[n] _____.

   When you lift weights for exercise, each act of going again is called one _____.

4. List as many words as you can think of that begin with the prefix *in* as it is defined in this exercise.

## EXERCISE IV—Inference

*Complete the sentences by inferring information about the italicized word from its context.*

1.  The auditor suspected that the city treasurer was guilty of *malfeasance* when he discovered that the treasurer had...

2.  Marty was still comatose, but the doctor said that movement of his fingers was an *auspicious* sign that Marty would probably...

3.  Danielle considers the painting to be the *apotheosis* of contemporary art, but Kurt...

## EXERCISE V—Critical Reading

*Below is a reading passage followed by several multiple-choice questions similar to the ones you will encounter on your SAT. Carefully read the passage and choose the best answer to each of the questions.*

*The following passage, entitled "The American Invasion," is one of Oscar Wilde's many astute observations of life during the Victorian period. In this essay, the famous satirist and dramatist comments on the spread of American culture to London, including such elements as Buffalo Bill's Wild West Show and the appearance of Cora Brown-Potter, an American of high society, who abandoned class expectations to become an actress.*

A terrible danger is hanging over the Americans in London. Their future and their reputation this season depend entirely on the success of Buffalo Bill and Mrs. Brown-Potter. The former is certain to draw; for English people are far more interested in American barbarism than they are in American civilization. When they
5   sight Sandy Hook they look to their rifles and ammunition; and, after dining once at Delmonico's, start off for Colorado or California, for Montana or the Yellow Stone Park. Rocky Mountains charm them more than riotous millionaires; they have been known to prefer buffaloes to Boston. Why should they not? The cities of America are inexpressibly tedious. The Bostonians take their learning too sadly; culture with
10  them is an accomplishment rather than an atmosphere; their "Hub," as they call it, is the paradise of prigs. Chicago is a sort of monster-shop, full of bustle and bores. Political life at Washington is like political life in a suburban vestry. Baltimore is amusing for a week, but Philadelphia is dreadfully provincial; and though one can dine in New York one could not dwell there. Better the Far West with its grizzly
15  bears and its untamed cowboys, its free open-air life and its free open-air manners,

its boundless prairie and its boundless mendacity! This is what Buffalo Bill is going to bring to London; and we have no doubt that London will fully appreciate his show.

With regard to Mrs. Brown-Potter, as acting is no longer considered absolutely essential for success on the English stage, there is really no reason why the pretty bright-eyed lady who charmed us all last June by her merry laugh and her nonchalant ways, should not—to borrow an expression from her native language—make a big boom and paint the town red. We sincerely hope she will; for, on the whole, the American invasion has done English society a great deal of good. American women are bright, clever, and wonderfully cosmopolitan. Their patriotic feelings are limited to an admiration for Niagara and a regret for the Elevated Railway; and, unlike the men, they never bore us with Bunkers Hill. They take their dresses from Paris and their manners from Piccadilly, and wear both charmingly. They have a quaint pertness, a delightful conceit, a native self-assertion. They insist on being paid compliments and have almost succeeded in making Englishmen eloquent. For our aristocracy they have an ardent admiration; they adore titles and are a permanent blow to Republican principles. In the art of amusing men they are adepts, both by nature and education, and can actually tell a story without forgetting the point—an accomplishment that is extremely rare among the women of other countries. It is true that they lack repose and that their voices are somewhat harsh and strident when they land first at Liverpool; but after a time one gets to love those pretty whirlwinds in petticoats that sweep so recklessly through society and are so agitating to all duchesses who have daughters. There is something fascinating in their funny, exaggerated gestures and their petulant way of tossing the head. Their eyes have no magic nor mystery in them, but they challenge us for combat; and when we engage we are always worsted. Their lips seem made for laughter and yet they never grimace. As for their voices they soon get them into tune. Some of them have been known to acquire a fashionable drawl in two seasons; and after they have been presented to Royalty they all roll their R's as vigorously as a young equerry or an old lady-in-waiting. Still, they never really lose their accent; it keeps peeping out here and there, and when they chatter together they are like a bevy of peacocks. Nothing is more amusing than to watch two American girls greeting each other in a drawing-room or in the Row. They are like children with their shrill staccato cries of wonder, their odd little exclamations. Their conversation sounds like a series of exploding crackers; they are exquisitely incoherent and use a sort of primitive, emotional language. After five minutes they are left beautifully breathless and look at each other half in amusement and half in affection. If a stolid young Englishman is fortunate enough to be introduced to them he is amazed at their extraordinary vivacity, their electric quickness of repartee, their inexhaustible store of curious catchwords. He never really understands them, for their thoughts flutter about with the sweet irresponsibility of butterflies; but he is pleased and amused and feels as if he were in an aviary. On the whole, American girls have a wonderful charm and, perhaps, the chief secret of their charm is that they never talk seriously except about amusements. They have, however, one grave fault—their mothers. Dreary as were those old Pilgrim Fathers who left our shores more than two centuries ago to found a New England beyond the seas, the Pilgrim Mothers who have returned to us in the nineteenth century are drearier still.

65 Here and there, of course, there are exceptions, but as a class they are either dull, dowdy or dyspeptic. It is only fair to the rising generation of America to state that they are not to blame for this. Indeed, they spare no pains at all to bring up their parents properly and to give them a suitable, if somewhat late, education. From its earliest years every American child spends most of its time in correcting the faults of its father and mother; and no one who has had the opportunity of watching an American family on the deck of an Atlantic steamer, or in the refined seclusion of
70 a New York boarding-house, can fail to have been struck by this characteristic of their civilization. In America the young are always ready to give to those who are older than themselves the full benefits of their inexperience. A boy of only eleven or twelve years of age will firmly but kindly point out to his father his defects of manner or temper; will never weary of warning him against extravagance, idleness,
75 late hours, unpunctuality, and the other temptations to which the aged are so particularly exposed; and sometimes, should he fancy that he is monopolizing too much of the conversation at dinner, will remind him, across the table, of the new child's adage, "Parents should be seen, not heard." Nor does any mistaken idea of kindness prevent the little American girl from censuring her mother whenever it is
80 necessary. Often, indeed, feeling that a rebuke conveyed in the presence of others is more truly efficacious than one merely whispered in the quiet of the nursery, she will call the attention of perfect strangers to her mother's general untidiness, her want of intellectual Boston conversation, immoderate love of iced water and green corn, stinginess in the matter of candy, ignorance of the usages of the best Baltimore
85 Society, bodily ailments, and the like. In fact, it may be truly said that no American child is ever blind to the deficiencies of its parents, no matter how much it may love them.

Yet, somehow, this educational system has not been so successful as it deserved. In many cases, no doubt, the material with which the children had to deal was
90 crude and incapable of real development; but the fact remains that the American mother is a tedious person. The American father is better, for he is never seen in London. He passes his life entirely in Wall Street and communicates with his family once a month by means of a telegram in cipher. The mother, however, is always with us, and, lacking the quick imitative faculty of the younger generation, remains
95 uninteresting and provincial to the last. In spite of her, however, the American girl is always welcome. She brightens our dull dinner parties for us and makes life go pleasantly by for a season. In the race for coronets she often carries off the prize; but, once she has gained the victory, she is generous and forgives her English rivals everything, even their beauty.
100 Warned by the example of her mother that American women do not grow old gracefully, she tries not to grow old at all and often succeeds. She has exquisite feet and hands, is always *bien chaussée et bien gantée* and can talk brilliantly upon any subject, provided that she knows nothing about it.

Her sense of humour keeps her from the tragedy of a grande passion, and, as
105 there is neither romance nor humility in her love, she makes an excellent wife. What her ultimate influence on English life will be it is difficult to estimate at present; but there can be no doubt that, of all the factors that have contributed to the social revolution of London, there are few more important, and none more delightful, than the American Invasion.

1.  As used in line 5, *Sandy Hook* refers to
    A.  an actress disliked by Americans.
    B.  an actress disliked by the British.
    C.  one of the first landmarks seen by travelers to America.
    D.  a species of buffalo found in New England.
    E.  the name of a popular frontier lodge that caters to tourists.

2.  As used in line 11, a *prig* is probably
    A.  someone who exaggerates propriety or conformity.
    B.  a Washington bureaucrat on leave.
    C.  a broken stick.
    D.  an animal that subsists on beans.
    E.  someone who dismisses education for experience.

3.  *Delmonico's* (line 6) was the paragon of fine American restaurants at the
    time this article was written. The author mentions the eatery because it
    A.  demonstrates that America, though primitive, has distinct cultural
        elements.
    B.  is a courteous advertising gesture for the new restaurant.
    C.  dispels myths that Americans prefer seafood to steak.
    D.  proves that the American frontier begins in New York.
    E.  suggests the irony of the people who want to travel to the wild
        frontier.

4.  The *vestry* mentioned in line 12 would probably resemble a
    A.  blacksmith.
    B.  neighborhood homeowners' association.
    C.  university lecture.
    D.  Congressional hearing.
    E.  tailor shop.

5.  Which of the following choices identifies an implication in the first line
    of paragraph 2?
    A.  Mrs. Brown-Potter will be a hit.
    B.  Most actors are conceited.
    C.  Mrs. Brown-Potter is not an impressive actress.
    D.  Mrs. Brown-Potter is charming, but she will not succeed.
    E.  Few interior decorators are as competent as Mrs. Brown-Potter.

6. The author suggests that American women are entertaining because they
   A. appreciate London's rich history.
   B. they are cryptic and unpredictable.
   C. rarely visit London.
   D. are diligent workers.
   E. constantly talk about historic battles.

7. In line 63, *they* probably refers to
   A. young Americans.
   B. university professors.
   C. the upper class.
   D. American mothers.
   E. tourists arriving in London.

8. The description of child-parent relationships in paragraph 3 is
   A. an extended pun, because it plays on the word *parents*.
   B. unnecessary because it detracts from the passage and makes no sense.
   C. ironic because it exchanges the roles of parents and children.
   D. an example of personification.
   E. the thesis of the passage.

9. The author of the passage probably feels that
   A. America produces good actors, but not good chefs.
   B. American culture is an abomination to self-respecting Londoners.
   C. too many people are attracted to American pastimes.
   D. American culture is ridiculous but entertaining.
   E. America is a threat to the British way of life.

10. When this passage was written, the intended audience was probably
    A. the American public.
    B. British citizens.
    C. the Queen of England.
    D. people who followed Cora Brown-Potter.
    E. anyone watching the play.

# Lesson Nineteen

1. **insuperable** (in sōō′ pər ə bəl)  *adj.*  not able to be overcome
The *insuperable* tide dragged the swimmer away from the shore.
*syn: indomitable; invulnerable*

2. **apex** (ā′ peks)  *n.*  the highest point of something
The *apex* of Mt. Everest is the highest point in the world.
*syn: acme; pinnacle; summit*  *ant: bottom*

3. **acrid** (a′ krəd)  *adj.*  marked by a sharp taste or smell; bitter
The burning plastic produced *acrid* fumes.

4. **fulminate** (ful′ mə nāt)  *v.*  to voice disapproval or protest
The crowd *fulminated* about destroying a historical landmark to make
room for a shopping mall.
*syn: denounce*

5. **jejune** (ji jōōn′)  *adj.*  without interest; dull
Allen abandoned his *jejune* life on the farm to become a racecar driver.
*syn: insipid; routine*  *ant: interesting; dramatic*

6. **hegemony** (hi je′ mə nē)  *n.*  influence or domination over
The Spanish explorers claimed *hegemony* over the native peoples of
Latin America.
*syn: dominion; reign*

7. **truculent** (trək′ yə lənt)  *adj.*  marked by ferocity
Only one brave warrior volunteered to battle the *truculent* dragon.
*syn: ravenous; savage*  *ant: tame; gentle*

8. **credulity** (kri dōō′ lə tē)  *n.*  willingness to believe too readily
Kim expressed *credulity* for claims of alien abductions despite the
absence of any real evidence.
*syn: faith; credence*  *ant: skepticism*

9. **dross** (dros)  *n.*  refuse or waste
Landfills are filling rapidly, so communities must find a new way to dispose of *dross*.
*syn: trash*

10. **verisimilitude** (ver ə sə mi′ lə tüd)  *n.*  the appearance of truth
The *verisimilitude* of the forged documents almost fooled the experts.
*syn: authenticity; realism*

11.   **viscous**   (vis´ kəs)   *adj.*   having a thick or sticky consistency like glue
Mixing water and flour creates a *viscous* substance that is similar to paste.
*syn: glutinous; adhesive*

12.   **psychosomatic**   (sī kō sə ma´ tik)   *adj.*   of or relating to symptoms caused by mental or emotional problems
The doctor refused to prescribe medication for Jane's *psychosomatic* headaches.

13.   **abnegation**   (ab ni gā´ shən)   *n.*   unwillingness to admit reality or truth; denial
Maria was in a state of *abnegation* when she found out her husband had died in a car accident.
*syn: rejection*                                        *ant: acceptance; admission*

14.   **polyglot**   (pä´ lē glät)   *n.*   someone with knowledge of two or more languages
The Latin professor was a *polyglot* who spoke six different languages.

15.   **gravitas**   (gra´ və täs)   *n.*   seriousness
The judge's *gravitas* helped to increase the severity of the case.
*syn: weightiness*

## EXERCISE I—Words in Context

*From the list below, supply the words needed to complete the paragraph. Some words will not be used.*

| | | | |
|---|---|---|---|
| truculent | apex | hegemony | viscous |
| abnegation | fulminate | credulity | dross |

1. Jim's parents _____ at his naive _____ in conspiracy theories. "Why do you fill your head with such _____?" his mother asked. "You and dad are just minions to the government's _____," said Jim. When the _____ aliens arrive and turn you into slaves, you'll reconsider my so-called _____."

*From the list below, supply the words needed to complete the paragraph. Some words will not be used.*

| | | | |
|---|---|---|---|
| acrid | abnegation | gravitas | verisimilitude |
| viscous | insuperable | apex | |

2. The black, _____ tar on the roof caught fire when lightning struck the _____ of the metal weathervane. The flames spread throughout the shed, finally igniting a pile of tires and filling the air with _____ smoke. The fire became _____ by the time the flames reached the office; the fire department did not have the equipment to control it. No one realized the _____ of the situation until the gas line beneath the office exploded, sending a fireball high into the air.

*From the list below, supply the words needed to complete the paragraph. Some words will not be used.*

| | | |
|---|---|---|
| psychosomatic | apex | polyglot |
| acrid | jejune | verisimilitude |

3. Dr. Kerry, a[n] _____ who speaks four ancient languages, was enjoying the _____ day raking leaves when his cellular phone rang. It was Dr. Orris, another archaeologist, and he wanted Dr. Kerry to look at an artifact that had the _____ of an ancient Mayan relic. Dr. Kerry reluctantly agreed, but first he went to the dermatologist to determine whether his newest skin abrasion was _____ or the consequence of touching poison oak leaves.

## EXERCISE II—Sentence Completion

*Complete the sentence in a way that shows you understand the meaning of the italicized vocabulary word.*

1. Most of the people thought that the prisoner was innocent, so they *fulminated* when the judge…

2. Sean's *psychosomatic* headaches occurred whenever he remembered…

3. Victoria reached the *apex* of her career early in life, and now she feels as though her career is…

4. The *polyglot* is an excellent spy because she…

5. The president of the corporation sought economic *hegemony* over…

6. The autographed photo had the *verisimilitude* of a genuine item, but it…

7. It surprised everyone when, in the third round, the *insuperable* boxer…

8. Sophia did not realize the *gravitas* of Joe's condition until she saw that he had…

9. Kevin briefly experienced *abnegation* when he realized that his lottery ticket had…

10. Unless you want the *acrid* taste of powdered cement in your mouth, you should wear a mask when we begin to…

11. The wounded dog was so *truculent* that the veterinarian was forced to…

12. Rebecca used the *viscous* epoxy to…

13. Tim cleaned the fish for dinner and threw the *dross*…

14. Ben had *credulity* for the existence of bigfoot, but none of his friends…

15. The speaker tried to enhance his usually *jejune* lectures by…

## EXERCISE III—Roots, Prefixes, and Suffixes

*Study the entries and answer the questions that follow.*

The roots *apt* and *ept* mean "fit."
The roots *aster* and *astr* mean "star."
The root *capit* or *cap* means "head."
The prefix *dis* means "apart" or "not."
The suffix *al* means "pertaining to."

1. Using literal translations as guidance, define the following words without using a dictionary.

   A. adaptable      D. asterisk
   B. adept          E. captain
   C. astral         F. decapitate

2. A *disaster* is a misfortune or a calamity. Write a possible explanation as to why the word *disaster* contains a root that means *star*.

3. A[n] _____ pupil might have personal interests that fit a particular subject.
   An inept worker might not be _____ for a particular job.

4. In a *capitalist* economy, citizens are the _____ of their own *capital*, or wealth.

5. List as many words as you can think of that contain the roots *apt* or *ept*.

6. List as many words as you can think of that contain the roots *aster* or *astro*.

## EXERCISE IV—Inference

*Complete the sentences by inferring information about the italicized word from its context.*

1. The noisy mob *fulminated* outside the courthouse because it did not agree with...

2. The *credulity* that you give to supermarket tabloids is absurd because they are...

3. Becky had difficulty getting the *viscous* pancake syrup from the container because it...

## EXERCISE V—Writing

*Here is a writing prompt similar to the one you will find on the writing portion of the SAT.*

Plan and write an essay based on the following statement:

Caring is the greatest thing, caring matters most.
–Last words of Friedrich Von Hugel
(1852-1925)

**Assignment:** Do you agree or disagree with Von Hugel's opinion about caring? Write an essay in which you support or refute Von Hugel's statement. Support your point with evidence from your own reading, classroom studies, and personal observation and experience.

**Thesis:** Write a one-sentence response to the above assignment. Make certain this single sentence offers a clear statement of your position.

*Example: Friedrich Von Hugel's last words form a pleasant idea, but it is doing—not caring—that truly matters most.*

**Organizational Plan**: If your thesis is the point on which you want to end, where does your essay need to begin? List the points of development that are inevitable in leading your reader from your beginning point to your end point. This list is your outline.

**Draft**: Use your thesis as both your beginning and your end. Following your outline, write a good first draft of your essay. Remember to support all your points with examples, facts, references to reading, etc.

**Review and revise**: Exchange essays with a classmate. Using the Holistic scoring guide on page 244, score your partner's essay (while he or she scores yours). If necessary, rewrite your essay to correct the problems indicated by the essay's score.

## Improving Paragraphs

*Read the following passage and then answer the multiple-choice questions that follow. The questions will require you to make decisions regarding the revision of the reading selection.*

1    Long workdays can be depressing, especially when it means arriving at work before daylight and leaving after dark. People in the northernmost parts of the United States endure this endless nightlife all winter long and now, doctors have found that a consistent lack of sunlight has negative psychological effects on people; however, life without daylight does indeed cause depression. The most vulnerable people in the United States are, of course, those who live in Alaska, where residents experience only several hours of dim sunlight during the winter months.

2    Anchorage natives have adapted to short days and long nights, but adapting is a real problem for people who are new to the state. Winters are difficult enough in the pipeline city; subfreezing temperatures and snow merely enhance the entrapping effect of the unending winter darkness. During the winter in Anchorage, the sun does not rise until 10:15 a.m., well after people have arrived at work. The sun goes down at 3:45 p.m., and most people still have another hour or two of work before they can leave.

3    The Trans-Alaskan Pipeline, an 800-mile artery of Alaska, employs nearly one thousand workers, many of whom work around-the-clock shifts. The occupational stress from working swing shifts, combined with the lack of vacation opportunities during the long winters, increases the probability of depression for the Alaskan workers. Winter is a tough time for animals, too, because they frequently get run over on unlighted roadways.

4    Like animals in hibernation, people suffering from Seasonal Affective Disorder (SAD), overeat and sleep most of the day. They have trouble concentrating and functioning at work and in personal relationships. Victims of SAD often suffer disastrous economic consequences when depression prevails over the desire to properly maintain finances. Many sufferers declare bankruptcy or lose their jobs.

5    An estimated one in four people suffer from SAD in Alaska. The depression is so prevalent that therapists report not having the resources to help all the people who seek treatment.

1. Which of the following changes would correct an error in paragraph 1?
   A. Replace *people* with *citizens*.
   B. Capitalize *northernmost*.
   C. Delete *of course*.
   D. Change *psychological* to *mental*.
   E. Delete *however*.

2. Which of the following changes would best clarify the topic of the passage?
   A. Expound on the problems that animals have during Alaskan winters, and explain why animals can also develop SAD.
   B. Introduce SAD in the first paragraph, and use the supporting paragraphs to explain the effects of the condition on people in Alaska.
   C. Include a paragraph about North Pacific weather patterns, and explain how precipitation can amplify the symptoms of SAD.
   D. Eliminate any information about workdays.
   E. Include information on how to treat Seasonal Affective Disorder.

3. Which of the following should be deleted from paragraph 3?
   A. sentence 1
   B. sentence 2
   C. sentence 3
   D. the word *unlighted*
   E. the word *opportunities*

4. Which of the following paragraph arrangements would improve the logical order of the passage?
   A. 1, 2, 3, 4, 5
   B. 1, 2, 4, 3, 5
   C. 1, 3, 2, 4, 5
   D. 2, 3, 4, 5, 1
   E. 1, 5, 3, 4, 2

5. Which of the following would be the most appropriate concluding sentence for the passage?
   A. Therefore, people should make it a point to get out into the sun more often.
   B. For people and animals alike, Seasonal Affective Disorder will be a challenge to face for years to come.
   C. Therapists should appeal to the government for additional funding and employees.
   D. Therapists will probably notify the Alaskan Pipeline officials of their discoveries.
   E. Perhaps, in the distant future, Alaska will build another pipeline—a pipeline that brings sunshine from California.

# Lesson Twenty

1.  **intractable** (in trak´ tə bəl)  *adj.*  difficult to manipulate or govern
    It took the blacksmith several days to hammer the *intractable* iron rods into elaborate railings.
    *syn: unmanageable; rigid*

2.  **disseminate** (di se´ mə nāt)  *v.*  to disperse or scatter
    Health officials *disseminated* flyers to warn people about deer ticks.
    *syn: distribute*

3.  **sinecure** (sī´ ni kyur)  *n.*  a job that provides income but requires little or no work
    The company employees were so autonomous and productive that the manager's job was a *sinecure*.

4.  **tendentious** (ten den´ chəs)  *adj.*  biased in perspective; preferring one view over another
    The journalist's *tendentious* article about the incident angered many readers.
    *syn: jaundiced; partisan*                                *ant: indifferent*

5.  **politic** (pä´ lə tic)  *adj.*  prudent or shrewdly tactful
    Ashley's *politic* manners made her an excellent lawyer and negotiator.
    *syn: sagacious; cunning*

6.  **extemporaneous** (ek stem pə rā´ nē əs)  *adj.*  done without planning; spur of the moment; unexpected; makeshift
    William made *extemporaneous* repairs to the roof to stop the leak.
    *syn: impromptu; spontaneous*

7.  **discursive** (dis ker´ siv)  *adj.*  jumping from one topic to another without any order or reason
    The scientist had so many ideas that his lectures tended to be *discursive* and difficult to follow.
    *syn: digressive; rambling*

8.  **diaspora** (dī as´ pə rə )  *n.*  a dispersion of people from their homeland
    Native American groups experienced a *diaspora*, and few ever recovered their lands.
    *syn: displacement*

9. **requiem** (re´ kwē əm)  *n.*  a religious service or song for the deceased
The church held a *requiem* after the death of one of its parishioners.

10. **traduce** (trə dōōs´)  *v.*  to slander someone's reputation
Anthony's one time friend now *traduced* his name around campus because of his disgraceful behavior.
*syn: smear; besmirch*

11. **acerbic** (ə ser´ bik)  *adj.*  sarcastic in mood, tone, or temper; harsh
The *acerbic* shopkeeper offended the customers and caused a drop in sales.

12. **beatitude** (bē a´ tə tōōd)  *n.*  a state of happiness or joy
The parents lived in *beatitude* in the hours following the birth of their first child.
*syn: bliss; euphoria*                               *ant: agony*

13. **maladroit** (ma lə droit´)  *adj.*  not resourceful or cunning; inept
After his original plan failed, the *maladroit* captain could not decide what to do next.
*syn: incompetent*

14. **androgynous** (an drä´ jə nəs)  *adj.*  having features of both sexes; suitable for both male and female
The *androgynous*-looking hats are designed to be worn by both men and women.

15. **augur** (o´ gər)  *n.*  someone who predicts future events according to omens
The mysterious *augur* was watchful for ominous signs whenever he was faced with an important choice.
*syn: clairvoyant; oracle*

## EXERCISE I—Words in Context

*From the list below, supply the words needed to complete the paragraph. Some words will not be used.*

| | | | |
|---|---|---|---|
| maladroit | augur | disseminate | sinecure |
| extemporaneous | beatitude | discursive | |

1.  Brian experienced a[n] _____ when he was offered the job of night watchman. He hated hard work, and he assumed that the job would be a[n] _____ since he could recline in a chair during most of his shift.

    Brian's dream job lasted one day. During his first shift, the _____ security guard forgot to lock the door to the warehouse, and Brian was sleeping in his chair when workers arrived in the morning. The boss made a[n] _____ decision to fire Brian on the spot, and then he _____ a memo to the other security guards about taking their jobs seriously.

*From the list below, supply the words needed to complete the paragraph. Some words will not be used.*

| | | | |
|---|---|---|---|
| acerbic | discursive | politic | requiem |
| intractable | diaspora | androgynous | |

2.  The FBI found it nearly impossible to track the Gatliones—a crime family whose _____ throughout the United States made it _____. Some of its _____ bosses had created businesses that concealed criminal operations, and phone taps were useless because the FBI could not decode the _____ conversations between gangsters and their henchmen. Agents occasionally arrested the family's hired thugs, but their _____ attitudes made it clear that they weren't going to release any information that would incriminate their bosses.

*From the list below, supply the words needed to complete the paragraph. Some words will not be used.*

| | | | |
|---|---|---|---|
| acerbic | requiem | augur | beatitude |
| androgynous | traduce | tendentious | |

3. The choir, dressed in white, _____ robes, sang movements of the _____ that the late composer had written for his own funeral. Superstitious people had the _____ idea that the death should be blamed on a[n] _____ who had convinced the composer that a visit from a raven meant certain death. They thought that the old seer had caused the composer to worry himself to death. Angry citizens _____ the old oracle and eventually ran him out of town.

## EXERCISE II—Sentence Completion

*Complete the sentence in a way that shows you understand the meaning of the italicized vocabulary word.*

1. The community theater *disseminated* flyers that told people the...

2 Both sides gave their *tendentious* accounts of what happened, and neither of them was...

3. Many retired people find *sinecures* because they...

4. The Prussian general took the *intractable* men and turned them into...

5. Nelson was forced to give an *extemporaneous* speech when...

6. Irish families experienced a *diaspora* during the potato famine, and now their family names are found in...

7. The child's *discursive* explanation made it difficult for the detective to...

8. The *politic* investor knew that her stock would drop in value, so she...

9. The restaurant owner claimed that the food critic *traduced* him by...

10. Lanna appreciated the *beatitude* she felt during the church services until her little brother...

11. If you do not stop giving *acerbic* answers to your dad's questions, you will not be allowed to…

12. It was raining, so the *requiem* was held…

13. The king's *augur* warned him not to…

14. The *maladroit* waiter angered the customer by…

15. The *androgynous* hospital gowns were designed to…

## EXERCISE III—Roots, Prefixes, and Suffixes

*Study the entries and answer the questions that follow.*

The roots *neo* and *nova* mean "new."
The roots *tort* and *tort* mean "twist" or "bend."
The roots *reg*, *rig*, and *rect* mean "rule" or "govern."
The roots *cide* and *cis* mean "to kill."
The root *nat* means "to be born."
The root *phy* means "to grow."
The prefix *ex* means "out."
The prefix *de* means "off."

1. Using literal translations as guidance, define the following words without using a dictionary.

   A. direct          D. retort
   B. incorrigible    E. decide
   C. extort          F. excise

2. The rebels killed the dictator-king in an act of _____, because the king's _____ had brutally ruled the country.

   If you want to get into good physical shape, you must allow yourself to be ruled by a good exercise _____.

3. You will find newborn babies in the _____ ward of the hospital.

   A *neophyte* at a sport might lose to experienced players because he or she is _____ to the game.

4. A *novice* who lacks carpentry experience might have difficulty _____ a home, or "making it new again."

5. Some would say that it is lying to _____ the truth by bending facts.

   A[n] _____ can bend his own body beyond the usual limits of normal human flexibility. Medieval _____ devices were sometimes used to stretch or twist people for punishment.

## EXERCISE IV—Inference

*Complete the sentences by inferring information about the italicized word from its context.*

1. The automobile dealership fired the *maladroit* salesman because he could not...

2. If you want a large turnout at the bake sale, you should *disseminate* information about the event so that...

3. Eugene's poorly-prepared, *discursive* presentation confused everyone because it did not...

## EXERCISE V—Critical Reading

*Below is a pair of reading passages followed by several multiple-choice questions similar to the ones you will encounter on the SAT. Carefully read both passages and choose the best answer to each of the questions.*

*The following passages, by Benjamin Franklin (1706-1790) and Francis Bacon (1561-1626), respectively, offer two perspectives on personal finance.*

### Passage 1

When I was a child of seven years old, my friends, on a holiday, filled my pocket with coppers. I went directly to a shop where they sold toys for children; and being charmed with the sound of a *whistle*, that I met by the way in the hands of another boy, I voluntarily offered and gave all my money for one. I then came home, and
5  went whistling all over the house, much pleased with my *whistle*, but disturbing all the family. My brothers, and sisters, and cousins, understanding the bargain I had made, told me I had given four times as much for it as it was worth; put me in mind what good things I might have bought with the rest of the money; and laughed at me so much for my folly, that I cried with vexation; and the reflection gave me more
10  chagrin than the *whistle* gave me pleasure.

This, however, was afterwards of use to me, the impression continuing on my mind; so that often, when I was tempted to buy some unnecessary thing, I said to myself, *Don't give too much for the whistle;* and I saved my money.

As I grew up, came into the world, and observed the actions of men, I thought I
15  met with many, very many, *who gave too much for the whistle.*

When I saw one too ambitious of court favor, sacrificing his time in attendance on levees, his repose, his liberty, his virtue, and perhaps his friends, to attain it, I have said to myself, *This man gives too much for his whistle.*

When I saw another fond of popularity, constantly employing himself in politi-
20  cal bustles, neglecting his own affairs, and ruining them by that neglect, *He pays, indeed*, said I, *too much for his whistle.*

If I knew a miser, who gave up every kind of comfortable living, all the pleasure of doing good to others, all the esteem of his fellow-citizens, and the joys of benevolent friendship, for the sake of accumulating wealth, *Poor man*, said I, *you pay too*
25  *much for your whistle.*

When I met with a man of pleasure, sacrificing every laudable improvement of the mind, or of his fortune, to mere corporeal sensations, and ruining his health in their pursuit, *Mistaken man*, said I, *you are providing pain for yourself, instead of pleasure; you give too much for your whistle.*

30  If I see one fond of appearance, or fine clothes, fine houses, fine furniture, fine equipages, all above his fortune, for which he contracts debts, and ends his career in a prison, *Alas!* say I, *he has paid dear, very dear, for his whistle.*

When I see a beautiful sweet-tempered girl married to an ill-natured brute of a husband, *What a pity, say I, that she should pay so much for a whistle!*

35    In short, I conceive that great part of the miseries of mankind are brought upon them by the false estimates they have made of the value of things, and by their *giving too much for their whistles.*

Yet I ought to have charity for these unhappy people, when I consider that, with all this wisdom of which I am boasting, there are certain things in the world so
40    tempting, for example, the apples of King John, which happily are not to be bought; for if they were put to sale by auction, I might very easily be led to ruin myself in the purchase, and find that I had once more given too much for the *whistle.*

## Passage 2

RICHES are for spending, and spending for honor and good actions. Therefore extraordinary expense must be limited by the worth of the occasion; for voluntary undoing may be as well for a man's country as for the kingdom of heaven. But ordinary expense ought to be limited by a man's estate; and governed with such regard,
5    as it be within his compass; and not subject to deceit and abuse of servants; and ordered to the best show, that the bills may be less than the estimation abroad. Certainly, if a man will keep but of even hand, his ordinary expenses ought to be but to the half of his receipts; and if he think to wax rich, but to the third part. It is no baseness for the greatest to descend and look into their own estate. Some for-
10    bear it, not upon negligence alone, but doubting to bring themselves into melancholy, in respect they shall find it broken. But wounds cannot be cured without searching. He that cannot look into his own estate at all, had need both choose well those whom he employeth, and change them often; for new are more timorous and less subtle. He that can look into his estate but seldom, it behooveth him to turn all
15    to certainties. A man had need, if he be plentiful in some kind of expense, to be as saving again in some other. As if he be plentiful in diet, to be saving in apparel; if he be plentiful in the hall, to be saving in the stable; and the like. For he that is plentiful in expenses of all kinds will hardly be preserved from decay. In clearing of a man's estate, he may as well hurt himself in being too sudden, as in letting it run
20    on too long. For hasty selling is commonly as disadvantageable as interest. Besides, he that clears at once will relapse; for finding himself out of straits, he will revert to his customs: but he that cleareth by degrees induceth a habit of frugality, and gaineth as well upon his mind as upon his estate. Certainly, who hath a state to repair, may not despise small things; and commonly it is less dishonorable to abridge petty charges, than to stoop to petty gettings. A man ought warily to begin charges which once begun will continue; but in matters that return not he may be more magnificent.

1.    As used in line 9 of the first passage, *vexation* most nearly means
    A.  sadness.
    B.  aggravation.
    C.  anger.
    D.  jealousy.
    E.  equity.

2.  According to passage 1, which of the following examples does *not* qualify as "giving too much for a whistle?"
    A.  ruining one's ears by listening to loud music
    B.  going bankrupt after purchasing a lavish home
    C.  spending large amounts of money on gambling
    D.  getting married before purchasing a home
    E.  getting fired after stealing money from the workplace

3.  The term *court favor* in line 16 of the first passage refers to
    A.  popularity.
    B.  judges.
    C.  criminals.
    D.  dating.
    E.  sportsmanship.

4.  In passage 1, the author uses a whistle as a metaphor for a
    A.  tangible good.
    B.  marketplace.
    C.  want.
    D.  person.
    E.  child's toy.

5.  As used in line 5 of the second passage, *compass* most nearly means
    A.  argument.
    B.  liking.
    C.  maximum.
    D.  range.
    E.  misfortune.

6.  According to passage 2, one's routine expenses should not exceed
    A.  one-third of his income.
    B.  one-half of his income.
    C.  his income.
    D.  the cost of the servants' salaries.
    E.  the value of the estate.

7.  Which of the choices is the most appropriate title for passage 2?
    A.  Pay Less For Your Whistle
    B.  Putting Your Money To Work
    C.  Saving is Essential
    D.  Spending Wisely
    E.  Perceiving Value

8. Which of the choices best paraphrases the following line from passage 2?

> A man had need, if he be plentiful in some kind of expense, to be as saving again in some other.

A. A penny saved is a penny earned.
B. People who have considerable debt should eliminate trivial expenses.
C. A person who spends a lot of money on one thing needs to be frugal about other things.
D. People should open savings accounts if they spend too much money.
E. Spending too much money for one thing will limit one's ability to purchase other things.

9. Which of the lines from passage 2 has the most similar meaning to the following example from passage 1?

> When I met with a man of pleasure, sacrificing every laudable improvement of the mind, or of his fortune, to mere corporeal sensations, and ruining his health in their pursuit, *Mistaken man,* said I, *you are providing pain for yourself, instead of pleasure; you give too much for your whistle.*

A. Riches are for spending, and spending for honor and good actions. (line 1)
B. A man had need, if he be plentiful in some kind of expense, to be as saving again in some other. (line 15)
C. For he that is plentiful in expenses of all kinds will hardly be preserved from decay. (line 17)
D. In clearing of a man's estate, he may as well hurt himself in being too sudden, as in letting it run on too long. (line 18)
E. A man ought warily to begin charges which once begun will continue; but in matters that return not he may be more magnificent. (line 25)

10. Which of the choices best describes the difference in intent between the passages?
A. Passage 1 focuses on money while passage 2 focuses on property.
B. Passage 1, unlike passage 2, suggests a change in lifestyle.
C. Passage 1 emphasizes value while passage 2 emphasizes thrift.
D. Passage 1 emphasizes frugality, while passage 2 emphasizes profit.
E. Passage 1 is witty while passage 2 is dull.

# Lesson Twenty-One

1. **bon mot**  (bōn mō´)  *n.*  a witty remark or saying
   Jerry ended every meeting with a *bon mot* about work productivity.
   *syn: quip*

2. **peon**  (pē´ än)  *n.*  various laborers who are generally landless
   The farmer hired *peons* to work his fields during the summer months.
   *syn: serf; servant*

3. **plutocrat**  (plōō´ tə krat)  *n.*  a member of the controlling upper-class
   Thomas Jefferson was a *plutocrat* who helped to shape America's government.
   *ant: plebian*

4. **plenary**  (plē´ nə rē)  *adj.*  complete in every way; full
   With the arrival of the bride, the wedding was *plenary* and could finally begin.
   *syn: thorough; entire*                    *ant: incomplete; lacking*

5. **digress**  (dī gres´)  *v.*  to deviate from the original subject or course
   The professor usually *digressed* from his original topic during his class lectures.
   *syn: stray*

6. **furlough**  (fər´ lō)  *n.*  a leave of absence
   The soldier was granted a *furlough* after his heroic deeds.
   *syn: vacation; liberty*

7. **misogyny**  (mə sä´ jə nē)  *n.*  a hatred toward females
   People attribute Cody's *misogyny* to his jealousy of his sister's success.

8. **stolid**  (stä´ ləd)  *adj.*  showing or having little or no emotion; unemotional
   The *stolid* gambler revealed no clue that he was holding a winning hand.
   *syn: impassive; stoic*                    *ant: expressive; agitated*

9. **succor**  (sə´ kər)  *n.*  something that gives relief or aid
   The medicine will be *succor* for the ailing people.
   *syn: comfort; ease*                    *ant: aggravation; annoyance*

10. **travesty**  (tra´ və stē)  *n.*  poor representation or imitation; distortion
    The Broadway musical was a *travesty* of the original show of the same title.
    *syn: perversion; sham*

11. **xeric** (zir´ ik) *adj.* characterized by or adapted to a dry habitat
Do not add too much water to *xeric* plants such as cacti; they require very little.

12. **clandestine** (klan des´ tən) *adj.* marked by secrecy
Only trusted agents could attend the *clandestine* meeting of the rebels.
*syn: undercover; hidden*

13. **potboiler** (pät´ boi lər) *n.* a poorly done artistic work, often for quick profit
Critics described the novels as a series of *potboilers* with little literary value.

14. **redoubtable** (ri dau´ tə bəl) *adj.* arousing fear
The drill sergeant was known for his *redoubtable* demeanor with new recruits.
*syn: dreadful; dire*                    *ant: wonderful; fortunate*

15. **vignette** (vin yet´) *n.* a short, descriptive literary sketch
Harold's autobiography is a collection of *vignettes* about events in his life.

## EXERCISE I—Words in Context

*From the list below, supply the words needed to complete the paragraph. Some words will not be used.*

| | | | |
|---|---|---|---|
| vignette | redoubtable | succor | plenary |
| digress | clandestine | xeric | furlough |

1.  Even the _____ creatures and people of the desert were unaware of the _____ testing facility deep beneath the sand and soil. Constructed as a countermeasure to the _____ threat of biological weapons, the hidden facility featured a[n] _____ laboratory in which scientists could identify and exploit organisms without the risk of contaminating the public. Some of the researchers were leading professors who had taken _____ from their teaching duties. Program managers ensured that research did not _____ from the mission of the laboratory—to minimize the threat of biological agents in the United States.

*From the list below, supply the words needed to complete the paragraph. Some words will not be used.*

| | | | |
|---|---|---|---|
| peon | xeric | bon mot | potboiler |
| plutocrat | stolid | succor | travesty |
| vignette | misogyny | plenary | |

2.  A six-dollar tub of popcorn was Meredith's only _____ while she watched the lousy _____ at the movie theater. The film made a[n] _____ of the book on which it was based, mostly because it omitted the best _____ from the original story. In the book, the central character is a[n] _____ who suffers under the _____ of a wealthy heiress who wants to rid her estate of any women other than herself. The servant becomes _____ after years of emotional abuse, and she dies alone and penniless. In the movie, the peasant woman becomes a wealthy _____ after discovering that her real father left her an enormous inheritance. The script is loaded with modern clichés and _____ that do not belong in the movie's seventeenth-century setting.

## EXERCISE II—Sentence Completion

*Complete the sentence in a way that shows you understand the meaning of the italicized vocabulary word.*

1. The knight had a *redoubtable* reputation on the battlefield because he…

2. No one noticed the *clandestine* camera because it looked like…

3. The remake of the classic film was a *travesty* of the original because…

4. The *stolid* judge showed no reaction to the witness, even when she…

5. Dr. Hafner, the creative writing professor, took a *furlough* from his duties in order to…

6. The wrongfully imprisoned woman received a *plenary* pardon when police found evidence that…

7. The king ordered the *peons* to construct a…

8. The trailer for the new movie featured a *vignette* in which the lead character…

9. The movie sequel was a *potboiler* that used the popularity of the first film to…

10. The *xeric* vegetation required…

11. The air-dropped rations were *succor* for the…

12. Grandpa's *misogyny* was apparent by the way he treated…

13. At this time, I'd like to *digress* from the topic of art to…

14. Some believe that *plutocrats* create laws that benefit only…

15. The detective on the police drama series recited a tacky *bon mot* every time he…

# EXERCISE III—Roots, Prefixes, and Suffixes

*Study the entries and answer the questions that follow.*

The root *plic* means "to fold."
The root *domin* means "lord" or "master."
The prefixes *com* and *con* mean "together" or "very."
The prefix *im* means "in."
The roots *vince* and *vict* mean "to conquer" or "to defeat."
The prefix *e* means "from" or "out."
The prefix *in* means "against" or "not."
The prefix *pre* means "in front of" or "before."

1. Using literal translations as guidance, define the following words without using a dictionary.

   A.  evict          D.  invincible
   B.  convict        E.  predominate
   C.  convince       F.  province

2. The animal that controls the other animals in a group is often called the
   _____ animal.

   If no one can take control of a person, then that person is said to be
   _____.

   If you become the master of a group, then you _____ it.

3. The word *implicate* means "to connect incriminatingly," or "to connect to a crime." Originally, *implicate* meant "to entangle," or "to interweave." Explain why a word that once meant "to entangle" has come to mean "to connect to a crime."

4. If someone increases the number of folds in a situation, then he or she is said to _____ matters.

   When someone gives *explicit* instructions, he or she _____ the information to make it understandable.

   If you are into the folds of a subject, then you have a[n] _____ understanding of it.

5. List as many words as you can think of that contain the roots *vince* or *vict*.

## EXERCISE IV—Inference

*Complete the sentences by inferring information about the italicized word from its context.*

1. No one knew the cause of Steve's *misogyny*, but it was apparent when he worked around women because he...

2. The *stolid* cowboy did not even flinch when...

3. The company phone list contained the numbers to a few key personnel, but the president wanted a *plenary* list that...

## EXERCISE V—Writing

*Here is a writing prompt similar to the one you will find on the writing portion of the SAT.*

Plan and write an essay based on the following statement:

> Emily Dickinson wrote, "There is no frigate like a book / To take us to lands far away." One book I've read that "transported" me to distant lands was

> _____.

**Assignment:** Write an essay in which you discuss the book that you named. Explain how the book opened up an unexplored world for you, and if and how it changed the way in which you think or perceive. Support all your claims and assertions with detailed and accurate references to the book that you are discussing.

**Thesis:** Write a one-sentence response to the above assignment. Make certain this single sentence offers a clear statement of your position.

*Example: Though it is a fictitious universe with its own internal logic, J.R.R. Tolkien's Middle Earth is so perfectly crafted that the adventures of hobbits, elves, dwarves, and humans in* <u>The Lord of the Rings</u> *are as vivid and real to me as they would be if I were observing them in person.*

**Organizational Plan**: If your thesis is the point on which you want to end, where does your essay need to begin? List the points of development that are inevitable in leading your reader from your beginning point to your end point. This list is your outline.

**Draft**: Use your thesis as both your beginning and your end. Following your outline, write a good first draft of your essay. Remember to support all your points with examples, facts, references to reading, etc.

**Review and revise**: Exchange essays with a classmate. Using the Holistic scoring guide on page 244, score your partner's essay (while he or she scores yours). If necessary, rewrite your essay to correct the problems indicated by the essay's score.

## Identifying Sentence Errors

*Identify the grammatical error in each of the following sentences. If the sentence contains no error, select answer choice E.*

1. Even if I <u>was</u> invited, I <u>wouldn't have</u> gone to the <u>picnic</u>.      <u>No error</u>
   (A)      (B)                (C)                                    (D)              (E)

2. If I <u>had saved</u> enough <u>money</u>, I <u>would of</u> traveled to San Francisco <u>last year</u>.
            (A)              (B)        (C)                                        (D)
   <u>No error</u>
      (E)

3. <u>Jane</u> <u>enjoys</u> <u>to play</u> <u>the piano</u>.      <u>No error</u>
   (A)    (B)      (C)      (D)                (E)

4. <u>They're</u> running away <u>is</u> not <u>going to get</u> them out of trouble with <u>the law</u>.
   (A)                    (B)        (C)                                        (D)
   <u>No error</u>
      (E)

5. The doctor <u>she advised</u> me <u>to cut</u> <u>down on</u> salt.      <u>No error</u>
   (A)            (B)              (C)      (D)                          (E)

## Improving Sentences

*The underlined portion of each sentence below contains some flaw. Select the answer choice that best corrects the flaw.*

6. The woman Shakespeare wrote about in sonnet 130 must have been real special.
   A. The women Shakespeare wrote about in sonnet 130 must have been real special.
   B. The woman Shakespeare wrote about in "Sonnet 130" must have been very special.
   C. The woman whom Shakespeare wrote about in Sonnet 130 must have been real special.
   D. The woman Shakespeare wrote about in "Sonnet 130" must have been real special.
   E. The woman Shakespeare wrote about in sonnet 130 must have been very special.

7. One student which is in our class asked What does this poem mean?
   A. One student who is in our class asked What does this poem mean?
   B. One student which is in our class, asked What does this poem mean?
   C. One student who is in our class, asked "What does this poem mean?"
   D. One student which is in our class, asked "What does this poem mean"?
   E. One student who is in our class asked, "What does this poem mean?"

8. How come all these pomes was about love death and time.
   A. How come all these poems were about love death and time.
   B. Why all these poems was about love, death, and time?
   C. How come all these poems were about love, death and time?
   D. Why were all these poems about love death and time.
   E. Why were all these poems written about love, death, and time?

9.  Many modern readers recognize the quotation, <u>No man is an island, but they don't know that it is a line from Donne's meditation seventeen.</u>
    A.  ...No man is an island, but they don't know that it is a line from Donne's meditation seventeen.
    B.  ..."No man is an island," but they do not know that it is a line from Donne's "Meditation 17."
    C.  ..."No man is an island," but they don't know that it is a line from Donne's meditation seventeen.
    D.  ..."No man is an Island", but they don't know that it is a line from Donnes' Meditation 17.
    E.  ...No man is an island, but they don't know that it is a line from Donne's meditation seventeen.

10. Many people no longer <u>except the customs, and beliefs</u> of the Renaissance.
    A.  accept the customs and beliefs
    B.  accept the customs, and beliefs
    C.  except the customs or beliefs
    D.  except the beliefs and customs
    E.  accept the beliefs and the customs

# REVIEW

## Lessons 15 – 21

### EXERCISE I – Sentence Completion

*Choose the best pair of words to complete the sentence. Most choices will fit grammatically and will even make sense logically, but you must choose the pair that best fits the idea of the sentence.*

*Note that these words are not taken directly from lessons in this book. This exercise is intended to replicate the sentence completion portion of the SAT.*

1. If you interpret the science-fiction novel literally, you will come to the _____ that the author believes in the _____ of UFOs.
   A. idea, possibility
   B. possibility, studying
   C. inevitability, theory
   D. conclusion, existence
   E. treatise, reality

2. The _____ atmosphere that prevailed on the ship prior to its departure quickly turned to _____ after passengers became ill from food poisoning, and the cruise had to be shortened.
   A. happy, unhappiness
   B. festive, rancor
   C. amazing, depression
   D. angry, hostility
   E. carnival, relief

3. Scientists, in order to examine their _____ about primate intelligence, subjected various apes and chimpanzees to a[n] _____ of carefully planned tests.
   A. hypothesis, battery
   B. feelings, sequence
   C. assumptions, conglomeration
   D. principles, structure
   E. knowledge, arrangement

4.  No amount of _____ or threats of expulsion by the principal could persuade the _____ , lazy student to apply himself.
    A.  assurances, indolent
    B.  pleading, argumentative
    C.  coercion, recalcitrant
    D.  rewards, rebellious
    E.  discipline, sorrowful

5.  Before the desert air heats _____ , few reptiles in the undergrowth are actually stirring; their cold-blooded bodies need warmth to _____ .
    A.  earth, circulate
    B.  everything, eat
    C.  thoroughly, function
    D.  sufficiently, begin
    E.  up, feed

6.  Many of the latest techniques that police units are using to control individuals or _____ mobs rely on _____ rather than lethal force.
    A.  noisy, witnesses
    B.  large, infiltration
    C.  unruly, incapacitation
    D.  riotous, non-deadly
    E.  uncooperative, deadly

7.  Booby traps set along the _____ of the camp successfully prevented the entry of _____ soldiers.
    A.  placement, enemy
    B.  entirety, all
    C.  area, combative
    D.  diameter, spying
    E.  perimeter, unauthorized

8.  _____ candidates for the job are _____ to send applications to the director of personnel.
    A.  Concerned, requested
    B.  Qualified, encouraged
    C.  Interested, determined
    D.  Competent, returning
    E.  New, required

## EXERCISE II – Crossword Puzzle

*Use the clues to complete the crossword puzzle. The answers consist of vocabulary words from lessons 15 through 21.*

**Across**

1.  highest point
3.  gap
7.  relevant
10. to scold
12. damnation
14. outrageous
17. to disperse
18. inept
20. intangible
24. to slander
25. traitor
27. wrongdoing
28. leave of absence
29. prudent

**Down**

2.  landless laborer
3.  excessive pride
4.  appearance of truth
5.  to charm
6.  seriousness
8.  denial
9.  unemotional
11. to deviate
13. loud
15. to think
16. significant
19. to ease
21. finest example
22. deceptive

23. poor imitation
26. boredom

# Scoring Guide for the SAT Writing Test

## ORGANIZATION

**6 = Clearly Competent**
The paper is clearly **organized** around the central point or main idea.
The work is **free of surface errors** (grammar, spelling, punctuation, etc.).

**5 = Reasonably Competent**
The **organizational plan** of the paper is **clear, but not fully implemented.**
**Minor surface errors** are present, but they **do not interfere** with the reader's understanding of the work.

**4 = Adequately Competent**
The **organizational plan** of the paper is **apparent, but not consistently implemented.**
**Surface errors** are present, but they **do not severely interfere** with the reader's understanding.

**3 = Nearly Competent**
There is evidence of an **organizational plan.**
Surface errors are **apparent** and **begin to interfere** with the reader's understanding of the work.

**2 = Marginally Incompetent**
The **organizational plan** of the writing is obscured by **too few** details and/or **irrelevant** details.
Surface errors are **frequent and severe enough** to **interfere** with the reader's understanding of the work.

**1 = Incompetent**
There is **no clear organizational plan** and/or **insufficient material.**
Surface errors are **frequent** and **extreme**, and **severely interfere** with the reader's understanding of the work.

# Scoring Guide for the SAT Writing Test

## DEVELOPMENT

**6 = Clearly Competent**
There is **sufficient** material (details, examples, anecdotes, supporting facts, etc.) to allow the reader to feel he/she has read a full and complete discussion without notable gaps, unanswered questions, or unexplored territory in the topic. Every word, phrase, clause, and sentence is **relevant**, contributing effectively to the thesis.
The work is **free of surface errors** (grammar, spelling, punctuation, etc.).

**5 = Reasonably Competent**
There is **nearly sufficient** material for a full and complete discussion, but the reader is left with **a few unanswered questions**. There is no superfluous or **irrelevant** material.
**Minor surface errors** are present, but they **do not interfere** with the reader's understanding of the work.

**4 = Adequately Competent**
There is **nearly sufficient** material for a full and complete discussion, but the reader is left with **a few unanswered questions**. Irrelevant material is present.
**Surface errors** are present, but they **do not severely interfere** with the reader's understanding.

**3 = Nearly Competent**
There is evidence of an organizational plan. There are **too few** details, examples, anecdotes, supporting facts, etc.
Surface errors are **apparent** and **begin to interfere** with the reader's understanding of the work.

**2 = Marginally Incompetent**
The organizational plan of the writing is obscured by **too few** details and/or **irrelevant** details.
Surface errors are **frequent and severe enough** to **interfere** with the reader's understanding of the work.

**1 = Incompetent**
The writing sample **attempts** to discuss the topic but is **severely marred** because surface errors are **frequent** and **extreme**, and **severely interfere** with the reader's understanding of the work.

# Scoring Guide for the SAT Writing Test

## SENTENCE FORMATION AND VARIETY

**6 = Clearly Competent**

Sentences are **complete, grammatically correct**, and assist the reader in following the flow of the discussion. The use of a **variety** of sentence structures contributes to the effective organization of the work and the reader's understanding.

The work is **free of surface errors** (grammar, spelling, punctuation, etc.).

**5 = Reasonably Competent**

Sentences are **complete, generally correct**, and do not distract the reader from the flow of the discussion. There is evidence of a concerted effort to use a **variety** of structures.

**Minor surface errors** are present, but they **do not interfere** with the reader's understanding of the work.

**4 = Adequately Competent**

Sentences are **complete and generally correct**. There is evidence of a concerted effort to use a **variety** of structures.

**Surface errors** are present, but they **do not severely interfere** with the reader's understanding.

**3 = Nearly Competent**

Sentences are **generally complete and grammatically correct**, but there are errors that begin to distract the reader. Sentence structure might be accurate, but **dull or routine**.

Surface errors are **apparent** and **begin to interfere** with the reader's understanding of the work.

**2 = Marginally Incompetent**

Problems in **sentence structure** and **grammar** are **distracting**, and provide **little or no variety**.

Surface errors are **frequent and severe enough** to **interfere** with the reader's understanding of the work.

**1 = Incompetent**

Sentences are **riddled with errors**. There is **little or no variety** in sentence structure.

Surface errors are **frequent** and **extreme**, and **severely interfere** with the reader's understanding of the work.

# Scoring Guide for the SAT Writing Test

## WORD CHOICE

**6 = Clearly Competent**

The word choice is **specific, clear, and vivid**. Powerful nouns and verbs replace weaker adjective-noun/adverb-verb phrases. Clear, specific, and accurate words replace vague, general terms.

The work is **free of surface errors** (grammar, spelling, punctuation, etc.).

**5 = Reasonably Competent**

Word choice is **clear** and **accurate**. For the most part, the writer has chosen **vivid, powerful words and phrases**.

Sentences are **complete, generally correct**, and do not distract the reader from the flow of the discussion. There is evidence of a concerted effort to use a **variety** of structures.

**4 = Adequately Competent**

Word choice is **adequate**. For the most part, the writer has chosen **vivid, powerful words and phrases**.

**Surface errors** are present, but they **do not severely interfere** with the reader's understanding.

**3 = Nearly Competent**

Word choice is **inconsistent**.

Surface errors are **apparent** and **begin to interfere** with the reader's understanding of the work.

**2 = Marginally Incompetent**

Word choice is **generally vague** with a few attempts at vividness.

Surface errors are **frequent and severe enough** to **interfere** with the reader's understanding of the work.

**1 = Incompetent**

Word choice is **lazy, inexact**, and **vague**. The writer has either too limited a vocabulary, or has not sought the best words for the topic, audience, and purpose.

Surface errors are **frequent** and **extreme**, and **severely interfere** with the reader's understanding of the work.

# Scoring Guide for the SAT Writing Test

## HOLISTIC [1]

**6 = Clearly Competent**
The writing sample discusses the **topic effectively and insightfully**.

The paper is clearly **organized** around the central point or main idea. There is **sufficient** material (details, examples, anecdotes, supporting facts, etc.) to allow the reader to feel he/she has read a full and complete discussion without notable gaps, unanswered questions, or unexplored territory in the topic. Every word, phrase, clause, and sentence is **relevant**, contributing effectively to that idea.

The word choice is **specific, clear, and vivid**. Powerful nouns and verbs replace weaker adjective-noun/adverb-verb phrases. Clear, specific, and accurate words replace vague, general terms.

Sentences are **complete, grammatically correct**, and assist the reader in following the flow of the discussion. The use of a **variety** of sentence structures contributes to the effective organization of the work and the reader's understanding.

The work is **free of surface errors** (grammar, spelling, punctuation, etc.).

**5 = Reasonably Competent**
The writing sample discusses the **topic effectively**.

The **organizational plan** of the paper is **clear, but not fully implemented**. There is **nearly sufficient** material for a full and complete discussion, but the reader is left with **a few unanswered questions**. There is no superfluous or **irrelevant** material.

Word choice is **clear** and **accurate**. For the most part, the writer has chosen **vivid, powerful words and phrases**.

**Minor surface errors** are present, but they **do not interfere** with the reader's understanding of the work.

Sentences are **complete, generally correct**, and do not distract the reader from the flow of the discussion. There is evidence of a concerted effort to use a **variety** of structures.

[1]Adapted from materials appearing on www.collegeboard.com, the official website of the College Board.

4 = Adequately Competent
The writing sample **discusses the topic.**

The **organizational plan** of the paper is **apparent, but not consistently implemented.** There is **nearly sufficient** material for a full and complete discussion, but the reader is left with **a few unanswered questions.**
Word choice is **adequate.** For the most part, the writer has chosen **vivid, powerful words and phrases.**

**Surface errors** are present, but they **do not severely interfere** with the reader's understanding.

Sentences are **complete and generally correct.** There is evidence of a concerted effort to use a **variety** of structures.

3 = Nearly Competent
The writing sample **discusses** the **topic** but is **marred** by the following:

There is evidence of an **organizational plan.** There are **too few** details, examples, anecdotes, supporting facts, etc.

Word choice is **inconsistent.**

Sentences are **generally complete and grammatically correct,** but there are errors that begin to distract the reader. Sentence structure might be accurate, but **dull or routine.**

Surface errors are **apparent** and **begin to interfere** with the reader's understanding of the work.

2 = Marginally Incompetent
The writing sample **discusses** the **topic,** but the discussion is **marred** by the following:

The **organizational plan** of the writing is obscured by **too few** details and/or **irrelevant** details.

Word choice is **generally vague** with a few attempts at vividness.

Problems in **sentence structure** and **grammar** are **distracting,** and provide **little or no variety.**

Surface errors are **frequent and severe enough** to interfere with the reader's understanding of the work.

1 = Incompetent
>
> The writing sample **attempts** to discuss the topic but **is severely marred** by the following:
>
> There is **no clear organizational plan** and/or **insufficient material**.
>
> Word choice is **lazy, inexact,** and **vague**. The writer has either too limited a vocabulary, or has not sought the best words for the topic, audience, and purpose.
>
> Sentences are **riddled with errors**. There is **little or no variety** in sentence structure.
>
> Surface errors are **frequent** and **extreme**, and **severely interfere** with the reader's understanding of the work.